4/22

DISCARDED

To all my lovely friends and family
along the Amalfi Coast who still
keep the traditions of this delectable
citrus fruit well and truly alive.

Gennaro's
LIMONI

VIBRANT ITALIAN RECIPES CELEBRATING THE LEMON

GENNARO CONTALDO

Photography by David Loftus

Interlink Books

An imprint of Interlink Publishing Group, Inc.
Northampton, Massachusetts

First published in 2021 by

Interlink Books
An imprint of Interlink Publishing Group, Inc.
46 Crosby Street, Northampton, Massachusetts 01060
www.interlinkbooks.com

Library of Congress Cataloging-in-Publication Data available
ISBN 978-1-62371-860-2

Photographer: David Loftus
Publisher: Helen Lewis
Project editor: Sophie Allen
American edition editor: Leyla Moushabeck
Design: Laura Russell and Nikki Ellis
Cover design: Harrison Williams
Production manager: Phil Brown

Printed and bound in China
10 9 8 7 6 5 4 3 2 1

To download our 48-page full-color catalog, please visit our website at
www.interlinkbooks.com or send us an e-mail at info@interlinkbooks.com.

CONTENTS

INTRODUCTION

Lemons are precious to me; a symbol of my beloved homeland, they stir up fond memories of my childhood as well as having a wealth of uses.

Lemons cleanse, refresh, disinfect, preserve, and are an absolute essential in the home.

Lemons were and still are a part of daily life for the locals of the Amalfi Coast and even though I came to England 50 years ago, my addiction for this citrus fruit has never ceased. Obviously, I was not able to find the Amalfi variety back then in the UK, but I would always buy the best I could. And when friends and family came to visit, their suitcase would be full of the sweetest of lemons, the absolute best present to remind me of home.

I can recognize whether a lemon is from Amalfi or not—rub the skin and inhale— all of us from the region can tell. Of course, you don't have to use Amalfi lemons to make the recipes in this book, just buy the best unwaxed variety you can find.

It has been an absolute pleasure writing this book—lemons are part of me, my childhood and culture. Going to my hometown of Minori to shoot part of this book was a sheer joy; visiting the lemon groves, the growers themselves, and friends and family who shared their favorite lemon recipes with me. It was wonderful watching my friend Valentino make his famous limoncello, Gabriele from the local pastry shop who showed me how to make candied lemon peel, the chef at my favorite restaurant for his signature fish dish, Erminia for her delicious rabbit dish, and to the many others, I am truly blessed to know you all and thank you for keeping alive the traditions of this indispensable citrus fruit.

I hope you enjoy recreating the recipes in this book and love using lemons just as much as I do and, who knows, you may get addicted too and insist on carrying a lemon with you wherever you go!

The Amalfi Lemon

I know I'm biased but the Amalfi lemon, locally known as the *Sfusato Amalfitano*, is like no other: a huge, elongated-in-shape, knobbly, thick-skinned citrus fruit, but oh-so wonderfully sweet and aromatic, with a soft pith that can be eaten as well. In fact, no part of the lemon is ever wasted; even the leaves are used.

Lemon growing in this area has been a tradition and a way of life for a thousand years. Lemons were brought to the region from the Middle East in the tenth century, and over time, local farmers managed to cross them with local bitter oranges to produce what we know today as the Amalfi lemon. The rich, fertile volcanic soil and

favorable climatic conditions of the valleys made it ideal for this citrus fruit to grow so abundantly.

With Amalfi being an important maritime republic at the time, the lemons became a highly sought-after trade item as well as an excellent source of vitamin C for sailors during long voyages. By the nineteenth century, the Amalfi lemon had gained great economic and social value for the area, and transformation of the landscape was finally complete. The once-unproductive rural land above the coastal villages had, over time, been transformed into terraces of lemon cultivation using wood from local chestnut trees as supports for the plants, and irrigation systems were put in place. For generations, entire families owned terraces and oversaw the cultivation process from start to finish, for perfect lemons to be sold and exported. Although the favorable conditions allowed for the growth of wonderful lemons, the location of the terraces, being high up, meant that bringing the lemons down to sea level was an arduous task. Unfortunately, in those days, this job was assigned to the women, who were known as *portatrici di limoni*, or lemon carriers. Thankfully, this is no longer the case; it's a job that men now do, and most use some sort of transport for part of the way. As a young child, I remember seeing these women dressed in their long skirts, with huge baskets perched on their shoulders, carrying kilos and kilos of lemons all the way down the long, steep, and often rickety stone paths. Groups of women would often make the journey together and sing, but not classic melodies, rather stories they would tell each other in a sing-song way.

Cultivation of the Amalfi lemon is still carried out using the same traditional methods that have always been used, with strict rules and regulations in place, and each lemon is still picked by hand. The lemons have been given IGP status, which provides official confirmation that they were grown in the area under strict control.

You could say I was "weaned" on lemons—we always had lemons at home; they were a must not only in the kitchen but for all sorts of household and medicinal purposes. Studies show that the Amalfi lemon has a higher percentage of vitamin C compared to other lemon varieties and its peel has a greater aromatic potency.

The popularity of the Amalfi lemon is seen all over the area's coastal towns and villages, in the form of cakes, pastries, ice cream, and the famous granita, as well as in savory dishes. I remember, as a little boy, I would often help the owner of the local café to zest lemons for his granita so I could be rewarded with a cold glass at the end. Whenever I embarked on fishing trips, I would always bring a lemon so I could squeeze the juice onto some fresh limpets. And on my childhood adventures, if I grazed my leg or arm, lemon juice would act as a disinfectant. In fact, even now, I hardly ever leave the house without a lemon. It's a habit I have never grown out of!

9   Introduction

Lemons in the kitchen

I always start my day with a lemon, well a sliver of zest which I add to my espresso first thing in the morning. It gives the strong coffee a lovely subtle refreshing tang. It's a habit I picked up from home in Italy and have enjoyed ever since—even when I stay in hotels overnight, I will ask for a lemon or, more often than not, I will have brought one with me!

When you think of lemons in the kitchen, desserts naturally spring to mind and there are indeed so many wonderful lemon-enhanced ice creams, puddings, cakes, cookies, but lemons are also fantastic in savory dishes. From simply drizzling the juice onto freshly cooked fish to wrapping the fruit's leaves around cheese and meat, no part of the lemon is ever wasted. The spongy white pith is a simple culinary delight used in a salad of lemons often eaten during summer as a refreshing light meal. Pasta and risotto dishes with lemon are a popular choice on restaurant menus along the Amalfi Coast and the combination of parmesan and lemon is a match made in heaven! Once you try a simple lemon risotto, you will be hooked and I'm sure the temptation to squeeze a little juice over it—and a lot of other dishes, too—will become habit!

Often just a squeeze of lemon or freshly grated zest over a finished dish is all you need to liven up a meal. It is my preferred dressing for salads and cooked vegetables. Like most Italians, I enjoy a drizzle of lemon juice over a simple grilled steak and other meat dishes like a *Milanese* (pork or veal covered in breadcrumbs). It not only gives a kick to the meat, but brings out the flavor.

Lemon is a great addition to drinks, from adding a few drops of juice to water, to the ever-popular alcoholic drink *Limoncello*. Made with lemon rinds, this refreshing after-dinner drink is also used in a variety of cocktails.

Often, as kids, we didn't have access to many sweet treats, so when we wanted something sweet, my mother would thinly slice a lemon and sprinkle it with sugar. We would eat the lot—peel, pith, and flesh, and lick the sweet juices left on the plate! I call it *Dolce dei Poveretti* (poor man's dessert) and I still enjoy it today. It's a sweet, tangy, and a healthier dessert option.

Household lemons

Growing up, I never really remembered household detergents, but I do recall my mother and sisters using lemons to clean. I especially remember lemon juice was used to rub off stains on our copper pots and pans; it was also used to clean the sink and the wooden kitchen table.

Lemons have antiseptic properties so the juice makes an ideal natural bleach. Of course you would need a lot of lemons if you used this method for all your cleaning, but you can combine the juice with vinegar, another natural cleaner, and the pleasant citrus aroma will disguise the not-so-pleasant vinegar smell.

These days at home, when I have used lemon halves lying around, they are never thrown away, but put in the dishwasher on the top rack and run through a cycle—it will give off a lovely, subtle lemon fragrance and help your plates sparkle.

Half a lemon will keep your fridge smelling sweet and it will clean and sterilize your microwave, giving it a pleasant fresh smell.

I rub my wooden chopping boards with lemon juice after using them. And after handling strong-smelling foods like fish, garlic, or onion, I wash my hands with lemon juice.

Medicinal lemons

A lemon a day keeps the doctor away

My mother didn't believe much in modern medicine and made her own herbal potions for various minor ailments. One of her most loved ingredients was lemon, which we always kept at home, and she made sure I carried one when going out on my adventures.

At the slightest hint of a sniffle, out came the lemons and she would make *canarino*—hot water infused with thinly pared lemon rind. For a sore throat, she would make me gargle with water and lemon juice, and a grazed knee would be disinfected with a drop or two of lemon juice—it stung but it did the trick! If we had eaten too much, especially after large festive meals, a glass of lemon water was the perfect remedy to aid digestion and feel less bloated. Even headaches and fever would be relieved with warm lemon water.

My older sisters would apply lemon juice to their hair to give it extra shine as well as using it on their skin to help with blemishes, rashes, and even sunburn.

Lemons are packed full of vitamin C as well as an abundance of other vital nutrients necessary for wellbeing, and its natural antibacterial properties help to heal both outside and inside of the body.

It has become scientifically evident that lemons are good for you on so many levels—it can help relieve the effects of colds and flu, high blood pressure, diabetes, stokes, stress, tiredness, excema, arthritis, respiratory and digestive problems and can even help with weight loss. A glass of lemon water a day helps flush out toxins and boosts the immune system which could in turn prevent many ailments.

SMALL
PLATES

INSALATA DI FINOCCHIO E MELA CON RAGU CALDO AGLI AGRUMI

Fennel and apple salad with a warm citrus ragu

This simple salad is perfect just after Christmas when sweet clementines are still in season and you are in need of something light and refreshing after all the rich festive food! Delicious as part of an antipasto or a light meal served with some grissini (breadsticks). I like to make this with an apple variety native to southern Italy, called Annurca, but it will be equally delicious with whatever eating apples you like.

Serves 4–6

1 fennel bulb, thinly sliced (reserve the green
    fronds for garnish)
1 large apple, quartered, cored, and thinly sliced
    (peeled if you wish)
2 tbsp extra virgin olive oil, plus extra for drizzling
segments of 2 clementines, membranes removed
segments of ½ lemon, membranes removed,
    roughly chopped in small pieces
5 tbsp water
handful of shaved Parmesan cheese
sea salt and black pepper

Arrange the fennel and apple slices on a plate, sprinkle with salt, drizzle with the olive oil, and toss together well.

Place the clementine and lemon pieces in a small pan with the water over medium heat and cook for about 5 minutes until the fruit has softened and the liquid has reduced. Remove from the heat and drain any excess liquid.

Pour the citrus fruit over the fennel and apple slices, top with Parmesan shavings, drizzle with a little more olive oil, sprinkle with black pepper, and garnish with some of the green fennel fronds. Serve immediately.

INSALATA DI CECI
Chickpea salad

Chickpeas and lemon go really well together and this salad, which can be eaten warm or cold, is delicious for any occasion—it's perfect as part of an antipasto, served as part of a buffet at parties, or as a light meal. It's also very simple to prepare, but because it's made using dried chickpeas, check the recommended cooking time on the package, and remember you need to allow them to soak in water overnight.

Serves 4
1¼ cups (250 g) dried chickpeas
¼ tsp baking soda
1 rosemary sprig
1 thyme sprig
3 sage leaves
3 bay leaves
1 lemon, one half juiced and other thinly sliced
4 tbsp extra virgin olive oil
5 mint leaves, finely chopped
6 anchovy fillets
5½ oz (150 g) Taggiasca olives, pitted
½ red chili pepper, finely chopped
sea salt

Cover the dried chickpeas in plenty of cold water with the baking soda (this helps to soften the chickpeas and speeds up cooking time) and leave to soak overnight.

Tie the herbs together to make a bouquet garni. Drain the chickpeas and put them in a pan with the herbs and enough fresh cold water to cover. Bring to a boil, then reduce the heat, cover the pan with a lid, and gently simmer until the chickpeas are tender (check the time on your package).

When tender, drain the chickpeas, reserving some of the cooking water, and allow them to cool a little.

In a small bowl, combine the lemon juice, olive oil, 4 tablespoons of the cooking water, and a little salt.

Transfer the chickpeas to a large bowl, along with the mint, anchovy fillets, olives, lemon slices, and red chili. Pour over the dressing and mix well. This can be served immediately, but it will last in the fridge for a couple of days (bring it to room temperature before serving).

INSALATA DI MARE
Mixed seafood salad

Insalata di mare is very popular and eaten in all the coastal towns and villages of Italy. I love the different varieties of seafood that you get in this dish; it's a feast for the eyes and a pleasure to eat! Try to get the freshest seafood you can for maximum flavor. This serves 4 as an appetizer or 2 for a light lunch. All you need is some good bread to mop up the delicious juices.

Serves 2–4
pared rind of 1 unwaxed lemon
12 oz (350 g) octopus
7 oz (200 g) squid
9 oz (250 g) mussels, scrubbed clean, beards removed
8 razor clams
7 oz (200 g) raw, shell-on jumbo shrimp
3 tbsp extra virgin olive oil
2 tbsp lemon juice
a handful of flat-leaf parsley leaves, roughly chopped
1 garlic clove, finely sliced
¼ fresh red chili pepper, finely chopped
sea salt
lemon wedges, to serve

Place a pot of water with about 3 lemon rind parings over medium heat, bring to a boil, then with the help of tongs, dip the octopus tentacles into the boiling water for a few seconds. Do this a couple more times in order to curl up the tentacles. Then drop the entire octopus into the boiling water and leave to cook for about 45 minutes until tender.

Meanwhile, prepare the rest of the seafood. Place another pot of water with a couple more lemon parings over the heat, bring to a boil, and cook the squid for 17–20 minutes until tender.

Put the mussels in a separate saucepan (without liquid), cover with a lid, and cook over medium heat for 3–4 minutes until the shells open. Any unopened mussels must be discarded. When cool enough to handle, remove most of the mussels from their shells, leaving a few in their shells for decoration if desired.

continued on next page...

Put the clams and shrimp in a saucepan with a little water and another couple of lemon parings, cover with a lid, and cook over medium heat for about 2 minutes until the clams have opened up and the shrimp have turned pink. Strain the liquid through a fine sieve and set aside. Remove the shells from the shrimp and clams, which you can chop or leave whole. You can also leave a couple of clams in their shells for decoration if desired.

When the octopus and squid are cooked, drain and leave to cool. Chop the octopus into chunks and slice the squid into rings, reserving the tentacles.

Combine the extra virgin olive oil, lemon juice, some salt, the parsley, garlic, chili, and 2 tablespoons of the clam/shrimp cooking liquid to make a dressing.

Combine the seafood in a large bowl (setting aside any mussels or clams still in their shells) pour the dressing all over, and mix well. Arrange on a serving plate, top with the unshelled seafood, and serve with lemon wedges.

INSALATA DI SGOMBRO AFFUMICATO E AGRUMI CON SALSINA DI CAPPERI

Mackerel and citrus fruit salad with caper dressing

Slightly oily smoked mackerel combines really well with the fresh flavors of both orange and lemon, finished off with a caper and herb dressing and crunchy fennel. This Sicilian-inspired salad is quick to prepare as a deliciously healthy summer lunch or as part of an antipasto, served with lots of good bread to mop up the dressing.

Serves 2
7 oz (200 g) smoked mackerel fillet, skin removed
juice of ½ orange
juice of 1 lemon
segments of 1 orange, membranes removed
segments of 1 lemon, membranes removed
2½ tbsp capers, very finely chopped
3 tablespoons extra virgin olive oil
4 basil leaves, finely chopped
6 mint leaves, finely chopped
½ cup (50 g) julienned fennel

Flake the smoked mackerel into pieces. Arrange on a plate and drizzle with the orange and lemon juice. Add the orange and lemon segments.

Combine the capers, olive oil, basil, and mint and pour over the salad. Arrange the fennel on top and serve.

FRUTAS

PIZZA AL LIMONE CON SALSICCIA, MOZZARELLA E RUCOLA

Lemon-infused pizza with sausage, mozzarella, and arugula

On the Amalfi coast, where large, sweet lemons are in abundance, pizzas are made with slices of lemon and provola, a local smoked cheese. As Amalfi lemons are not easily obtainable, I decided to make an alternative lemon pizza with zest in the dough and in the topping, and a squeeze of juice on the arugula at the end. The combination of lemon, sausage, onion, and rosemary works really well, and the arugula sprinkled on top adds to the lovely lemony freshness—try it on different pizzas!

Makes 2 large or 4 smaller pizzas/Serves 4

For the dough
4 cups (500 g) white bread flour, plus extra for dusting
¼ oz (7 g) envelope instant yeast
1 tsp sea salt
zest of 2 unwaxed lemons
approx. 1⅓ cups (325 ml) lukewarm water

For the topping
3 tbsp extra virgin olive oil
1 large white onion, finely sliced
9 oz (250 g) Italian pork sausages, skins
    removed and meat crumbled
a few rosemary sprigs
2 balls fresh mozzarella (approx. 9 oz/250 g)
zest of 1 unwaxed lemon
2 handfuls of arugula
extra virgin olive oil
lemon juice
sea salt and freshly ground black pepper

First make the dough. Combine the flour, yeast, salt, and lemon zest, and gradually stir in enough of the lukewarm water to make a dough. Knead the dough for about 10 minutes, cover with a cloth, and leave to rest for about 30 minutes.

continued on next page...

Divide the dough into 2 or 4 pieces (depending on what size pizzas you are making) and knead each one on a lightly floured surface for about 2 minutes. Place on a lightly floured baking pan, cover with a cloth, and leave to rest in a warm place for about 1 hour or until doubled in size.

Meanwhile, make the topping. Heat the extra virgin olive oil in a frying pan, add the onion, and sweat for a couple of minutes over medium heat. Stir in the sausage meat, rosemary, and some salt and pepper, and continue to cook for a couple of minutes. Remove from the heat and set aside. Slice the mozzarella into small pieces and set aside.

Preheat the oven to 400°F (200°C).

Take each piece of dough and flatten to make a pizza base (as thin as you like), top with the sausage mixture, scatter with the pieces of mozzarella, grate the lemon zest all over it, and bake in the oven for about 10 minutes, or until the base is cooked and golden.

Toss the arugula in a little extra virgin olive oil and lemon juice. Remove the pizzas from the oven, top with dressed arugula, and serve.

BRUSCHETTA CON SALMONE AFFUMICATO E MASCARPONE AL LIMONE

Bruschetta with smoked salmon and lemon mascarpone

These make lovely appetizers or finger food for a party. You can make the bruschetta as large or small as you like. Creamy mascarpone cheese combines really well with lemon and is a perfect combination with smoked salmon.

Makes 4 large bruschette
4 slices smoked salmon (approx. 3½ oz/ 100 g)
zest and juice of 1 unwaxed lemon
3½ tbsp (100 g) mascarpone
5 tsp finely chopped dill
4 slices sourdough bread
pinch of sea salt
freshly ground black pepper

Drizzle the smoked salmon with a little of the lemon juice, sprinkle with a little black pepper, and set aside.

Whisk the mascarpone with about 4 teaspoons of the lemon juice, half the lemon zest, the dill, and a little salt until creamy. Taste and adjust the amount of juice and salt accordingly.

Toast the slices of sourdough. Place a slice of smoked salmon on each, and top with mascarpone. Or you could spread a little of the mascarpone on the bread and top with salmon. Sprinkle with the remaining lemon zest and serve.

PURE' DI CECI
Chickpea purée

This simple chickpea purée can be served as an accompaniment to meat or veggie dishes, as a dip, or spread on crostini as an appetizer or snack. It can be served hot or cold, and you can make it in advance and store it in the fridge for a couple of days (just gently reheat it or serve at room temperature).

Serves 4–6
1 cup (200 g) dried chickpeas
2 rosemary sprigs, one left whole,
    needles stripped from the other
2 parings of lemon rind and the juice of 1 lemon
5 anchovy fillets
1 small garlic clove
1 tbsp extra virgin olive oil
6 tbsp chickpea cooking water
approx. ⅔ cup (150 ml) water

Soak the chickpeas in plenty of water overnight.

Drain, then place the chickpeas in a saucepan with the whole rosemary sprig and lemon rind, cover with fresh water, bring to a boil, and simmer until very tender—check your package for cooking time.

When the chickpeas are tender, drain, reserving about 6 tablespoons of the cooking water, and discard the rosemary sprig and lemon rind.

Put the cooked chickpeas, cooking water, and the remaining ingredients, except the water, into a blender or food processor and blend, gradually adding the water, until you obtain a smooth consistency.

PINZIMONIO

Raw vegetables with herb and lemon dip

Pinzimonio is a classic light Italian antipasto dish of crunchy raw vegetables served with a simple dip of extra virgin olive oil, salt, and pepper, to which some add vinegar or lemon juice. To give it a bit of a colorful twist, I have added herbs that have been blanched to soften them, and of course I use lemon juice to liven it up! You can use whatever raw vegetables you prefer and don't have to use the ones I have suggested—try radishes, scallions, tender artichokes, Belgian endive, cucumbers, and whatever else you find at the market. For parties, serve a large plate of different, colorful veggies at the center of the table or as part of an antipasto. You could also serve additional dips, like Lemon Mayo and Simple salad dressing (page 182).

Serves 4
2 carrots, peeled and sliced lengthways into batons
2 celery sticks, halved and sliced into batons
1 fennel bulb, sliced lengthways into about 8 pieces
leaves of ½ trevisana (long narrow radicchio)
½ red pepper, deseeded and sliced
½ yellow pepper, deseeded and sliced
For the dip
2 handfuls of flat-leaf parsley leaves
2 handfuls of basil leaves
4 tbsp extra virgin olive oil
2 tbsp lemon juice
sea salt

Arrange the vegetables on a platter.

Put the parsley and basil in a small pan with a little water, bring to a boil, and blanch for a couple of minutes. Drain and place the herbs in a food processor, along with the extra virgin olive oil, lemon juice, and a little salt. Process until the herbs are chopped and everything is nicely amalgamated. Pour into a small bowl and serve with the prepared vegetables.

LIMONI RIPIENI AL FORNO DI VALENTINO

Valentino's baked filled lemons

This dish was made for me by my good friend Valentino who uses the best, freshest anchovies, wonderful Amalfi lemons, and local mozzarella to create an unusual, delicious antipasto. You may need a little more or less of the filling ingredients depending on the size of your lemons. Serve one or two lemon halves per person as an appetizer. Valentino's tip: while you can use ready-made dried breadcrumbs to top the lemons, they tend to burn more easily and your own mixture of fresh bread and thyme quickly fried will enhance the flavor.

Serves 2–4

2 lemons, washed and dried
12–16 fresh anchovies, heads removed and cleaned
approx. ½ oz (15 g) country bread, lightly toasted
4 cherry tomatoes, halved or quartered depending on size
2 oz (60 g) fresh mozzarella, cut into small cubes
extra virgin olive oil
1 large slice bread, crusts removed, and finely chopped
    to resemble breadcrumbs
a few thyme leaves
sea salt and freshly ground black pepper

Preheat the oven to 350°F (180°C).

Halve the lemons and squeeze out the juice. Place the fresh anchovies in a small bowl, pour over the lemon juice, add a pinch of salt, and leave to marinate for 15 minutes.

With a small sharp knife, remove any remaining flesh from the squeezed lemon halves and trim the bases so they can stand up. Line the bottom of each half with a small piece of the lightly toasted bread (this will absorb moisture from the other ingredients). Place a couple of anchovies in each lemon, then tomatoes, followed by mozzarella, drizzle with a little extra virgin olive oil, and then make another layer.

Heat a splash of extra virgin olive oil in a frying pan over low to medium heat, add the breadcrumbs, thyme, salt, and pepper and fry, stirring, for about 30 seconds to allow the flavors to infuse. Top the lemons with this breadcrumb mixture. Place the stuffed lemons on a baking dish, drizzle with a little olive oil, cover with foil, and bake for 10–12 minutes. Then remove the foil and continue to bake for an additional 5 minutes or until the mozzarella has melted and the breadcrumbs are golden. Remove from the oven and serve.

SARDINE AL CARPIONE

Lemon-marinated sardines with diced vegetables

Al carpione is a traditional way of marinating fish or meat. It was commonly used in times before fridges were invented, especially in the northern lakes region of Italy where freshwater fish was in abundance. Wine vinegar was typically used, but I find lemon juice is just as good and it acts as a preservative in the same way. Cooking *al carpione* continues, but not for preserving reasons, often to make a delicious antipasto, like this dish.

Serve 1–2 sardines per person
6 fresh sardines, headless but left whole
all-purpose flour, for dusting
8 tbsp mild olive oil
1 carrot, finely chopped
1 celery stick, finely chopped
¾ cup (70 g) finely chopped fennel
1 small red onion, finely chopped
½ red (or yellow or orange) pepper, finely chopped
¼ red chili pepper, finely chopped
6 cornichons, finely chopped
2½ tbsp capers
1 tbsp chopped flat-leaf parsley
juice of 1 lemon
sea salt

Pat the sardines dry with paper towels and dust with a little flour. Heat 6 tablespoons of the olive oil in a frying pan. When hot, add the sardines and fry for 2–3 minutes on each side until golden. Remove from the heat and drain on paper towels. Arrange on a serving plate.

In another frying pan, heat the remaining 2 tablespoons of oil and and add all the finely chopped vegetables, including the cornichons and capers. Fry, stirring, over medium to high heat for about 5 minutes until they are slightly soft, but still crunchy. Remove from the heat, season with a little salt to taste, stir in the parsley and lemon juice and, while the veggies are still hot, pour them over the sardines, covering the fish. Leave to cool at room temperature, then serve.

LIMONI RIPIENI ALLA CREMA DI TONNO

Tuna-filled lemons

Here's something different, which I am sure will impress! This is great served as a refreshing antipasto or as a delicious light lunch with some good bread. I have given you two ways of serving—either in slices, or you can fill lemon halves. If you are in a hurry, then I would go for the lemon halves.

Serves 2–4
2 lemons, washed and dried

For the filling
8 tsp lemon juice
scant 2 tbsp capers, finely chopped
4 pitted green olives, finely chopped or left whole
scant 1 cup (130 g) drained canned tuna (in oil)
scant ½ cup (100 g) ricotta
2 anchovy fillets, finely chopped
½ handful of flat-leaf parsley, finely chopped
sea salt and freshly ground black pepper

Trim the top of each lemon until you can see the flesh. With a small sharp knife, cut around the flesh and use a small scoop or teaspoon to remove all of the flesh—do this over a bowl to catch all the juice; you want 8 teaspoons of juice for the filling. Set aside.

Combine the filling ingredients and mix until smooth. Fill the lemon cavities with the mixture, packing it in well to avoid any gaps or air bubbles.

You can serve immediately or, to serve in slices, wrap the filled lemons tightly in foil and place in the freezer for an hour. Remove from the freezer, unwrap the foil and, with a very sharp knife, cut into slices and arrange on a serving dish. Leave for about 20 minutes at room temperature before serving.

SPIEDINI DI SCAMORZA IN FOGLIE DI LIMONE

Skewers of scamorza cheese wrapped in lemon leaves

This traditional antipasto is served all along the Amalfi coast; it is really simple, using just two ingredients, but very effective and delicious! The locals use provola, a cheese that is like a hard smoked mozzarella, but you can more easily find scamorza in Italian delis, which is very similar. The smokiness of the cheese and the subtle flavor of the lemon leaves is a winning combination. You can cook them using a grill pan, but if you've got a barbecue going, then it's an ideal option. I've made them into skewers, but you could also simply sandwich the cheese between two lemon leaves and grill them that way.

Makes 10 little parcels/enough for 2 skewers
7 oz (200 g) scamorza cheese
10 lemon leaves
1 lemon, thinly sliced

Cut the scamorza into 10 slices. Wrap each one in a lemon leaf and thread onto a couple of skewers, alternating with a lemon slice.

Heat a griddle or grill pan. When hot, place the skewers on the pan to char for a couple of minutes on each side, pressing gently with a spatula until the cheese begins to melt. Alternatively place the skewers on your barbecue and turn every couple of minutes as before.

Remove from the heat, slide off the skewers, and serve. Simply unwrap the cheese and eat with the charred lemon slices. Enjoy with a simple tomato salad, if desired.

POLPETTINE AL TONNO E LIMONE
Tuna and lemon balls

While I was testing the recipe for Filled Sardines (page 107) I also made these *polpettine* with the same filling mixture. They are so delicious—once you eat one, you can't stop, so perhaps you should increase the quantity! Delicious served as part of an antipasto or as a snack, and kids just love them.

Makes approx. 24
scant 1 cup (120 g) drained canned tuna
¼ cup (60 g) ricotta
2 tsp finely chopped flat-leaf parsley
2 anchovy fillets, finely chopped, rinsed if salted
heaped 1 tbsp capers, finely chopped
2 tbsp grated Parmesan
zest of 1 unwaxed lemon
5 tsp lemon juice
all-purpose flour, for dusting
2 eggs, beaten
dried breadcrumbs, for coating
vegetable or sunflower oil, for frying
sea salt and freshly ground black pepper

Combine the tuna, ricotta, parsley, anchovy fillets, capers, Parmesan, lemon zest, and juice to make a smooth but not runny mixture. Check for seasoning and if necessary, add a little salt and black pepper. Form the mixture into small balls, roughly the size of chocolate truffles. Then dust them in flour, dip into beaten egg, and coat in breadcrumbs.

Heat enough oil in a frying pan to come about ½ inch (1 cm) up the sides. When hot, fry the polpettine, in batches if necessary, for about 2 minutes, turning them around until golden all over. Remove and drain on paper towels. Serve immediately—but they are equally delicious eaten cold.

INSALATA DI PEPERONI AL LIMONE

Roasted pepper salad

This simple and delicious salad is often made in Italy during the summer when peppers are in abundance. I have given you the method for roasting them in the oven, but you could roast them in a grill pan or, even better, on a barbecue, which really enhances the flavor. I suggest you make this dish ahead of serving it, because the longer you leave it to marinate, the more delicious it becomes. Serve with good bread, as a topping for crostini, as part of an antipasto with cured meats, as a side dish, or with Turkey Burgers (page 131). The addition of lemon to the dressing tastes great, and its acidity helps you digest the peppers better.

Serves 2–4
3 peppers—red, yellow, orange
1 garlic clove, finely chopped
a small handful of flat-leaf parsley leaves, roughly chopped
2 tbsp extra virgin olive oil
juice of ½ lemon
sea salt

Preheat the oven to 425°F (220°C).

When the oven is hot, place the whole peppers in a roasting or ovenproof dish and roast until charred and softened, turning them from time to time. You will need to allow about 30–40 minutes, depending on the size of the peppers.

Remove from the oven and leave aside until cool enough to handle (but don't allow them to get cold, or the skin will become too tough to remove). Working over a bowl to catch the juices, remove the skin, stalk, and seeds. Set aside.

Chop the pepper into slices and arrange on a plate, along with the garlic and parsley. Sprinkle with some salt.

Combine the extra virgin olive oil, lemon juice, and any of the pepper juices and pour over the peppers. Leave to marinate for at least 30 minutes before serving.

INSALATA DI LIMONI D'AMALFI
Amalfi lemon salad

This simple salad is enjoyed along the Amalfi coast, where delicious sweet lemons grow in abundance. The pith on Amalfi lemons is so thick and spongy that locally this bit is known as "*pane*" (bread). The recipe originated in the area as *cucina povera* (poor people's cooking) because lemons grew everywhere and were cheaply and easily obtainable. I remember eating this refreshing salad when I was growing up and still enjoy it when I return to my home village. To get the authentic flavor of this salad, I recommend you try to get Amalfi lemons; other varieties may taste too sour.

Serves 2–4
1 large unwaxed Amalfi lemon or other good-quality lemon
4 mint leaves, roughly chopped
2 tbsp extra virgin olive oil
1 tbsp red wine vinegar
sea salt

Carefully remove the rind of the lemon (reserve the parings for another recipe or enjoy in an espresso), but leave the white pith. Cut the lemon into slices. Arrange the slices on a plate, sprinkle over some salt, and scatter with the mint leaves. Combine the extra virgin olive oil and vinegar, pour over the lemons, and serve.

VEGETABLES

TAGLIATELLE AL LIMONE
Tagliatelle with lemon

Pasta with lemon is very common along the Amalfi coast and it can be prepared in various ways, often simply with olive oil, lemon, and parsley. This is my favorite way, with chili and garlic. The addition of a little butter at the end makes the sauce lovely and creamy—perfect for the tagliatelle to absorb.

Serves 4
11 oz (320 g) tagliatelle
3 tbsp extra virgin olive oil
1 garlic clove, finely chopped
¼ red chili pepper, finely chopped
2 tbsp (25 g) butter
zest and juice of 1 unwaxed lemon
3 tbsp grated Parmesan cheese,
    plus extra for sprinkling
handful of flat-leaf parsley, finely chopped
sea salt

Bring a large saucepan of salted water to a boil, add the tagliatelle, and cook until al dente.

Meanwhile, heat the extra virgin olive oil in a large frying pan, add the garlic and chili, and sweat over medium heat for a minute or so. Add a ladleful of the pasta water, then the butter, and allow it to melt before adding the lemon juice.

Drain the tagliatelle and, using a pair of tongs, add it to the pan and mix well. Stir in the Parmesan and parsley. Serve immediately, sprinkled with the lemon zest and extra Parmesan, if desired.

MEZZELUNE AL LIMONE
Lemon and ricotta-filled pasta

Pasta filled with local ricotta and lemon is a popular dish on restaurant menus along the Amalfi Coast. *Mezzelune* simply means half-moon. These filled pasta parcels, served in a creamy, buttery lemon sauce, are hard to resist. You need a pasta machine to make them because the dough needs to be really thin.

Serves 4–6 (makes approx. 65)

For the pasta dough
1¾ cups (200 g) "0" pasta flour
2 large organic free-range eggs

For the filling
1 cup (250 g) ricotta
zest of 2 unwaxed lemons, plus extra for sprinkling
4 tsp lemon juice
2½ tbsp grated Parmesan cheese
sea salt and freshly ground black pepper

For the sauce
7 tbsp (100 g) butter
20 mint leaves (optional)
4 tsp lemon juice
scant ½ cup (40 g) grated Parmesan cheese,
    plus extra for sprinkling

First make the pasta dough. Put the flour in a large bowl or on a clean work surface, make a well in the center, and break in the eggs. With a fork, gradually mix the flour and eggs, then knead with your hands until you obtain a smooth dough. Shape into a ball, wrap in plastic, and leave to rest in the fridge for about 30 minutes.

Meanwhile, prepare the filling. Drain the ricotta of any liquid, then place in a bowl and combine with the lemon zest, lemon juice, grated Parmesan, and some salt and pepper.

Remove the dough from the fridge and divide into quarters, so you can work with one piece at a time. Rewrap the pieces you are not using in the plastic to prevent the pasta from drying out.

continued on next page...

Roll the piece of pasta through a pasta machine working through the settings until the pasta is paper-thin. Place the sheet of pasta on a lightly floured work surface and cut out circles with a 2½-inch (6 cm) round cutter and lightly brush the edges with a little water. Place a little filling in the center, fold over into a half-moon shape, pressing down with your fingers, then make small indentations with a fork around the sealed edge. Gather up all the pasta trimmings, re-roll, and repeat. Continue with the remaining dough pieces and filling.

When you have made all the mezzelune, bring a large saucepan of salted water to a boil and drop in the *mezzelune*, a few at a time, to cook for about 3½ minutes.

Meanwhile, make the sauce. Put the butter in a large frying pan with the mint leaves (if using) and allow to melt over medium to high heat then add the lemon juice.

Once the *mezzelune* are cooked, use a slotted spoon or spider strainer to lift them out of the water and place in the frying pan, along with a couple of tablespoons of the cooking water. Cook over a medium to high heat for a minute or so, shaking the pan. Add the Parmesan and gently mix. Remove from the heat and serve immediately with an extra sprinkling of Parmesan and lemon zest.

LASAGNE CON ZUCCHINE E BESCIAMELLA DI LIMONE

Zucchini lasagne with lemon bechamel sauce

Simple to prepare, this light vegetarian lasagne with a refreshing hint of lemon makes a perfect meal at any time. Delicious served with a mixed side salad.

Serves 4

12 oz (350 g) zucchini, thinly sliced lengthways
a little extra virgin olive oil, for brushing
1 x quantity Lemon Bechamel Sauce (page 184)
8–10 lasagne sheets (use oven-ready lasagne that
 doesn't need presoaking)
a few basil leaves
⅓ cup (30 g) grated Parmesan cheese
1 ball fresh mozzarella cheese, roughly chopped
grated lemon zest, to serve

Place a grill pan over medium heat. Lightly brush the zucchini slices with some extra virgin olive oil. When the pan is hot, cook the zucchini slices for a couple of minutes on each side until golden brown. Remove and set aside.

Preheat the oven to 400°F (200°C). Ready the bechamel sauce.

Spread a little of the sauce over the base of a 9- x 7-inch (23 x 18 cm) ovenproof dish, then cover with a single layer of lasagne sheets, place zucchini slices on top, scatter with a few basil leaves, add a layer of lemon sauce, and sprinkle some Parmesan and mozzarella pieces. Continue with these layers until you have used all the ingredients, finishing with sauce, mozzarella, and Parmesan. Cover the dish with foil and bake for 15 minutes. Remove the foil and continue to bake for a further 15 minutes until golden brown and bubbling.

Remove from the oven, leave to rest for 5 minutes, then serve with a little freshly grated lemon zest.

PASTA E CECI AL FINOCCHIETTO E LIMONE

Pasta and chickpeas with fennel and lemon

Pasta and chickpeas is a popular dish all over Italy—certainly one that reminds me of my childhood—especially during the winter when we used a lot of dried beans and peas to make hearty meals like this one. The tang of lemon combines so well with earthy chickpeas and I often find myself squeezing extra juice over my portion. Wild fennel is much used in Italian cooking but if you can't find any, or you find the taste too strong, then simply omit it. Make sure to leave enough time to soak the chickpeas.

Serves 4
1 cup (200 g) dried chickpeas
3 tbsp extra virgin olive oil
2 small carrots, finely chopped
2 garlic cloves, left whole and squashed
generous 1 cup (100 g) finely chopped fennel bulb
3 tbsp (20 g) chopped wild fennel fronds (optional)
thinly pared rind of 1 unwaxed lemon
7 oz (200 g) tagliatelle, broken into little pieces
sea salt and freshly ground black pepper

To serve
grated Parmesan cheese
1 unwaxed lemon, zested then quartered

Soak the chickpeas in plenty of cold water overnight.

The next day, heat the extra virgin olive oil in a large pot, add the carrots, garlic, and fennel bulb, and sweat over medium heat for 2–3 minutes. Drain the chickpeas and stir them into the pot, along with the wild fennel (if using) and lemon rind. Add about 7½ cups (1.8 liters) of water, bring to a boil, and simmer over medium heat until the chickpeas are cooked, about 2 hours (check the instructions on your package).

When the chickpeas are cooked, add some salt and pepper to taste, increase the heat to a boil, and add the pasta—you may need a little more boiling water. Cook until the pasta is al dente. A little liquid may remain, like a thick soup.

Remove from the heat and serve with grated Parmesan, freshly grated lemon zest, and the lemon quarters for squeezing.

FARFALLE CON CAPPERI E LIMONE

Farfalle with capers and lemon

Here's a very quick and easy summery pasta dish, one that's made with very few ingredients, but is extremely tasty. Make sure you use good-quality capers in salt, and carefully peel the lemon so you don't include the white pith. Best served with a simple tomato salad for a perfect no-fuss al fresco lunch or dinner. But it is of course delicious served at any time of the year—especially when you are in a hurry.

Serves 4
14 oz (400 g) farfalle
3½ tbsp capers in salt, rinsed and drained
pared rind of 1 unwaxed lemon and 4 tsp lemon juice
handful of flat-leaf parsley leaves
4 tbsp extra virgin olive oil
sea salt and freshly ground black pepper

Bring a large pot of salted water to a boil and cook the farfalle until al dente.

Meanwhile, very finely chop the capers, lemon peel, and parsley and combine with the extra virgin olive oil and lemon juice.

Drain the pasta, place in a large bowl, pour over the sauce, mix well, and serve immediately with a little freshly ground black pepper.

LINGUINE CON PESTO DI MELANZANE AL PROFUMO DI LIMONE

Linguine with lemon-infused eggplant pesto

The combination of eggplants and lemon works really well together in this delicious pasta dish. The sauce is made a little like a pesto, but I have only blended the eggplant, adding the rest of the ingredients afterwards so that the sliced almonds give a bit of a crunch to the dish.

Serves 4
1 lb 2 oz (500 g) eggplants
2½ tbsp grated Parmesan cheese, plus extra to serve
zest of 1 unwaxed lemon and 2 tsp lemon juice
⅓ cup (30 g) sliced almonds, toasted and roughly chopped
12 oz (350 g) linguine
10 mint leaves, finely chopped
sea salt and freshly ground black pepper

Preheat the oven to 425°F (220°C). Wash the eggplants, dry well, and prick all over with a fork. Place in the hot oven and bake for 30–40 minutes until soft. Remove from the oven and allow to cool. When cool enough to handle, cut the eggplants in half lengthways, scoop out the flesh, and discard the skins. Place in a sieve over a bowl and press with the back of a spoon to remove the excess water. Transfer to a food processor or blender and proces until you obtain a smooth consistency.

Scrape the purée into a large bowl and combine with the Parmesan, half the lemon zest, the lemon juice, almonds, and a sprinkle of salt and pepper.

Bring a large pot of salted water to a boil, add the linguine, and cook until al dente. Drain, reserving some of the cooking water.

Add a little of the pasta cooking water to the eggplant mixture, then with the aid of a pair of tongs, add the linguine and mint leaves. Mix well together and serve immediately with a sprinkling of Parmesan and the remaining lemon zest.

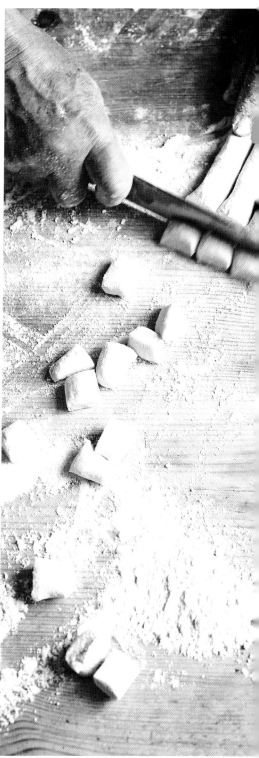

GNOCCHI AL LIMONE

Lemon gnocchi

Freshly made potato gnocchi are always a favorite in our household. The addition of a little lemon zest adds freshness and it marries well with the butter, mint, and lemon sauce. When we tested this recipe, I served it to the family for lunch; the gnocchi disappeared in seconds and I have never seen such clean plates!

Serves 4–6
2¼ lb (1 kg) starchy potatoes
2½ cups (300 g) all-purpose flour
1 large egg, beaten
zest and juice of 1 unwaxed lemon (juice reserved for the sauce)
rice flour, for dusting
sea salt

For the sauce
7 tbsp (100 g) butter
8 mint leaves, left whole
4 tsp lemon juice
⅓ cup (30 g) grated Parmesan cheese,
    plus extra to serve

To make the gnocchi, boil the potatoes in their skins until cooked, drain, allow to cool slightly, then remove the skins and mash. Combine with the flour, egg, a little salt to taste, and half of the lemon zest. Mix until you obtain a soft dough. Sprinkle a little rice flour over a work surface and roll out the dough into long sausage shapes. Using a sharp knife, cut into roughly ¾-inch (2 cm) lengths. Set aside.

Bring a large pot of lightly salted water to a boil. Drop the gnocchi into the water, in batches, and simmer for a minute or so until they rise to the top. Meanwhile, put the butter in a large frying pan with the mint leaves and lemon juice and melt over medium to low heat.

Remove the gnocchi with a slotted spoon and add it to the butter sauce with a little of the cooking water. Cook for a minute or so until all the gnocchi are coated in the sauce, add the Parmesan, mix well, and serve immediately with extra Parmesan and the remaining lemon zest.

RISOTTO AL FINOCCHIO E LIMONE

Fennel and lemon risotto

Fennel and lemon go really well together (see the pasta and chickpea recipe on page 58) and combine perfectly in a risotto. I have added the juice of a whole lemon into this recipe, giving it a lovely lemony flavor, but you could use less if you prefer. You could also add a knob of butter at the end, but I prefer to leave this risotto deliciously light.

Serves 2
approx. 3 cups (725 ml) hot vegetable stock
4 tsp extra virgin olive oil
1 banana shallot, finely chopped
generous 1 cup (100 g) finely sliced fennel bulb—include fronds
    if you like or use to garnish
¾ cup (140 g) risotto rice (carnaroli, vialone nano, or arborio)
zest and juice of 1 unwaxed lemon
a small handful of flat-leaf parsley, roughly chopped
3 tbsp grated Parmesan cheese, plus extra
    for sprinkling if desired
freshly ground black pepper

Place the vegetable stock in a saucepan over low heat to keep it warm.

In another pot, heat the extra virgin olive oil, add the shallot and fennel, and sweat over medium heat for a couple of minutes. Add the rice and stir with a wooden spoon to coat all the grains in the oil. Add some or all of the lemon juice and cook, stirring continuously, until the liquid is nearly all absorbed. Add a couple of ladlefuls of hot stock, stirring until absorbed, and continue adding and stirring for about 15 minutes until the rice is cooked—it should be soft on the outside but al dente in the center. (You may not need all of the stock, or you may need a little more.)

Remove from the heat and stir in the parsley and Parmesan. Serve immediately, scattered with lemon zest, black pepper, and extra Parmesan if desired.

CARCIOFI AL LIMONE

Braised lemon artichokes

This simple artichoke dish can be enjoyed as a side to most meat dishes or as a main course served with some good bread. Please don't be put off by the preparation of artichokes, once you've done one, you will know they are easy to prepare. The addition of lemon juice gives the artichokes a lovely tangy, fresh flavor.

Serves 4 as a side or 2 as a main
4 medium-sized globe artichokes
4 tbsp extra virgin olive oil
1 onion, finely sliced
1 tablespoon capers
handful of flat-leaf parsley, roughly chopped
juice of 2 lemons, plus a little extra
    for the acidulated water
sea salt and freshly ground black pepper

For the acidulated water, fill a medium-sized bowl with water, add a few drops of lemon juice, and set aside. This prevents the artichokes from turning black as you prepare them.

To prepare the artichokes, rinse under cold running water, then slice off the top quarter and most of the stem using a sharp knife. Use scissors to snip off the sharp thorns. Cut the artichokes into quarters, carefully remove and discard the hairy choke, and place them in the acidulated water until you are ready to use.

Drain the artichokes well, pat dry with a dish towel, and season well with salt and pepper. Heat the extra virgin olive oil in a large frying pan, add the artichokes, and stir-fry over high heat for 2–3 minutes until golden on all sides. Remove the artichokes and set aside. Add the onion to the same pan and sweat over medium heat for 3 minutes. Return the artichokes to the pan, along with the capers and parsley. Add the lemon juice and ½ cup (120 ml) water, bring to a boil, reduce the heat, and simmer with the lid on for about 10 minutes until the artichokes are tender and cooked through. Remove from the heat and serve.

VELLUTATA DI ZUCCA AL PROFUMO DI LIMONE

Pumpkin soup with lemon

Pumpkin and lemon is a winning combination, which I had never tried until my nephew in Italy told me how good it is. Now I always add a squeeze of lemon to this dish!

Serves 4
2 tbsp extra virgin olive oil
1 red onion, finely chopped
½ red chili pepper, finely chopped (optional)
1 lb 2 oz (500 g) cubed pumpkin
1 potato (approx. 5½ oz/150 g), peeled
    and chopped into small chunks
1 rosemary sprig, needles stripped and roughly chopped
3 cups (700 ml) hot vegetable stock
zest and juice of ½ unwaxed lemon

Heat the extra virgin olive oil in a medium-sized saucepan, add the onion and chili (if using), and sweat for a couple of minutes. Stir in the pumpkin, potato, and rosemary and sweat for a further 2–3 minutes. Add the hot stock, bring to a boil, then reduce the heat and simmer for 25–30 minutes until the pumpkin is soft. Blend to a creamy consistency, then stir in the lemon juice and serve with a sprinkle of the zest.

GRANO SPEZZATO AL PROFUMO DI LIMONE CON VERDURE

Lemon-infused bulgur with vegetables

Bulgur is cracked whole wheat grains and, like couscous, it absorbs the flavor of lemon juice beautifully. The addition of vegetables makes this a simple and healthy main course or you can serve it as an accompaniment to meat dishes.

Serves 2–4
1½ cups (200 g) bulgur
2 parings of lemon rind
zest of ½ unwaxed lemon
¼ cup (60 ml) lemon juice
3½ cups (800 ml) vegetable stock
3 tbsp extra virgin olive oil
2 garlic cloves, finely chopped
6 oz (180 g) zucchini, finely cubed
9½ oz (260 g) eggplant, finely cubed
6 baby plum tomatoes, quartered
6 mint leaves, finely chopped
sea salt

Place the bulgur, lemon rind, and vegetable stock in a saucepan, bring to a boil, and simmer for about 10 minutes until the liquid is absorbed and the bulgur is cooked—check the package instructions for timings.

Meanwhile, heat the extra virgin olive oil in a frying pan, add the garlic, and sweat for a minute. Add the zucchini, eggplant, and some salt, and stir over medium heat for about 10 minutes until tender but not mushy. About halfway through, stir in the tomatoes.

When the bulgur is cooked, remove from the heat, discard the rind, and stir in the lemon juice and mint. Stir in half the vegetables, place on a serving dish, top with the remaining vegetables, and sprinkle with freshly grated lemon zest.

FAGIOLINI CON LIMONE E BRICIOLE

Sautéed green beans with breadcrumbs and lemon

These beans make a delicious accompaniment to meat and fish dishes or the frittata on page 79. The breadcrumbs add bulk to the beans, so the recipe can even be enjoyed as a meal in itself.

Serves 2–4
7 oz (200 g) green beans, ends trimmed
2 tbsp extra virgin olive oil
1 banana shallot, finely sliced
juice of ½ lemon
4 mint leaves, roughly torn (optional)
3 tbsp dried breadcrumbs
sea salt and freshly ground black pepper

Bring a large pot of salted water to a boil, then add the green beans and simmer for about 7 minutes until tender. Drain and plunge into cold water—this will help retain the green color. Set aside.

Meanwhile, heat the extra virgin olive oil in a frying pan, add the shallot, and sweat for a couple of minutes until softened. Drain the green beans, add them to the frying pan, and stir for a couple of minutes over a high heat. Season with salt and pepper. Stir in the lemon juice, mint (if using), and breadcrumbs. Reduce the heat and mix well, cooking for just under a minute or so. Remove from the heat and serve.

FAGIOLI CANNELLINI CON VERDURE AL PROFUMO DI LIMONE

Lemon-infused cannellini beans with veggies

I love cooking dried beans, especially during the winter—I enjoy the ritual of pre-soaking the beans the night before in anticipation of cooking them the next day. Combined with some veggies, this makes a delicious main course and the addition of lemon juice gives it a nice refreshing kick. I usually use cannellini beans, but you can use whichever white beans you prefer. Always check the package instructions for cooking times.

Serves 4

1 ½ cups (300 g) dried cannellini or other white beans
2 tbsp extra virgin olive oil, plus extra for drizzling
1 carrot, finely chopped
½ red onion, finely chopped
1 celery stick, finely chopped
1 small zucchini, finely chopped
1 garlic clove, finely chopped
2 rosemary sprigs
3½ cups (800 ml) vegetable stock
a paring of lemon rind and juice of 1 lemon
freshly ground black pepper

Soak the dried beans in plenty of water and leave overnight. The next day, drain the beans, place in a saucepan, cover with cold water, bring to a boil, and cook for about 30 minutes until tender.

Meanwhile, heat the extra virgin olive oil in another large saucepan, add the carrot, onion, celery, zucchini, garlic, and rosemary and sweat over medium heat for about 5 minutes. Drain the beans and add to the veggies with the stock and lemon peel, bring to a boil, then reduce the heat, and continue to simmer until the beans are cooked, up to 25 minutes. About 5 minutes before the end of cooking time, stir in the lemon juice.

Remove from the heat and serve immediately with a drizzle of extra virgin olive oil and a grind of black pepper.

FRITTATA AL LIMONE
Lemon frittata

The delicate hint of lemon in this frittata comes first from marinating the onions in lemon juice and adding zest to the actual dish. Serve with a mixed salad and good bread as a tasty vegetarian main course.

Serves 4
14 oz (400 g) red onions, finely sliced
zest and juice of 1 unwaxed lemon
1½ tbsp (20 g) butter
3 tbsp extra virgin olive oil
generous 1 cup (250 ml) vegetable stock
6 eggs
handful of flat-leaf parsley, finely chopped
scant ½ cup (40 g) grated Parmesan cheese
sea salt and freshly ground black pepper

Place the onions in a bowl with the lemon juice and enough cold water to cover them. Set aside for 30–60 minutes, then drain well.

Heat the butter and 2 tablespoons of the extra virgin olive oil in a large nonstick frying pan, add the onions, and cook over low heat for 10 minutes, gently stirring. Pour in the stock and continue to cook gently for another 5–6 minutes until the liquid has been absorbed. Remove from the heat and cool slightly.

Meanwhile, beat the eggs then add the parsley, Parmesan, lemon zest, salt, and pepper. Stir in the onions.

Return the frying pan to the heat with 1 tablespoon of extra virgin olive oil, add the egg mixture, and cook gently for 5–7 minutes until the base is set. Carefully place a large plate over the pan and quickly invert the pan so that the frittata falls onto the plate, then slide it back into the pan to cook the other side. Alternatively, if you don't want to flip the frittata, place the frying pan under the broiler until golden brown. (You may need to protect the handle of your pan.) Serve hot or cold.

RISOTTO AL LIMONE

Lemon risotto

Tangy and creamy, this lovely risotto is quick and simple to prepare. When my kitchen cupboards are bare, this is my quick go-to meal. The rice absorbs the lemon juice and its flavor really comes through. I love the strong lemony taste, but if you prefer, use a little less lemon juice.

Serves 4
2 tablespoons extra virgin olive oil
3 tbsp (40 g) butter
1 small onion, finely chopped
½ celery stick, finely chopped
1½ cups (300 g) risotto rice (carnaroli, vialone nano, or arborio)
zest and juice of 2 unwaxed lemons
approx. 6⅓ cups (1.5 liters) hot vegetable stock
⅓ cup (30 g) grated Parmesan cheese,
    plus extra for sprinkling
sea salt and freshly ground black pepper
a small handful of basil leaves, roughly torn, to serve

Heat the extra virgin olive oil and half the butter in a pan, add the onion and celery, and sweat over medium heat for a couple of minutes until softened. Add the rice and stir with a wooden spoon until each grain is coated in the oil and butter. Stir in the lemon juice and cook, stirring continuously, until the liquid is nearly all absorbed. Add a couple of ladlefuls of hot stock, stirring until absorbed. Continue to do this for about 15–17 minutes until the rice is cooked—it should be soft on the outside but al dente in the center.

Remove from the heat, beat in the remaining butter, grated Parmesan, a little salt and pepper to taste, and lemon zest. Serve with freshly torn basil leaves and an extra sprinkling of grated Parmesan.

BROCCOLI ALL'AGLIO, PEPERONCINO E LIMONE

Broccoli with garlic, chili, and lemon

This is how I've always enjoyed lightly boiled vegetables, with some good extra virgin olive oil, garlic, chili, and lemon. This simple combination livens up the vegetables and makes a perfect side dish to meat and fish. I enjoy a plate of this on its own with lots of good bread.

Serves 4

1 lb 10 oz (750 g) broccolini
    or broccoli florets
2 tbsp extra virgin olive oil
1 garlic clove, very finely chopped
½ red chili pepper, finely chopped
zest and juice of ½ unwaxed lemon
sea salt

Place a pot of water over the heat, bring to a boil, and cook the broccoli for about 3 minutes until tender.

Meanwile heat the extra virgin olive oil in a frying pan, add the garlic and chili, and sweat for a minute. Using a slotted spoon or spider strainer, drain the broccoli and add it to the frying pan. Stir over medium heat for a couple of minutes and add the lemon juice and zest and a little salt to taste. Serve immediately.

ASPARAGI CON UOVA IN CAMICIA CON SALSINA AL BURRO E LIMONE

Asparagus with a creamy butter and lemon sauce and poached eggs

Butter, lemon, and Parmesan combine so well with this classic northern Italian dish of asparagus and eggs. Typically it is made without lemon, but the addition of both juice and zest really give this dish a pleasant kick. Serve with lots of good bread to mop up the delicious creamy juices. Ideal served as a brunch or light lunch.

Serves 2–4
1 lb 2 oz (500 g) asparagus
4 organic free-range eggs
7 tbsp (100 g) butter
zest of 1 unwaxed lemon and 3½ tbsp of juice,
    plus a little extra zest for sprinkling
⅓ cup (30 g) grated Parmesan cheese,
    plus a little extra for sprinkling
freshly ground black pepper

Snap off the hard stems of the asparagus and wash the stalks under cold running water. Place in a pot with some water, bring to a boil, and cook until just tender, 2–3 minutes, depending on the thickness of your asparagus.

At the same time, put a second pot of water over the heat and, when it boils, carefully crack the eggs into the water (or into a cup first) and poach for 3–4 minutes until the whites are set but the yolks are still nice and runny.

When the asparagus is ready, drain and place on a clean dish towel to dry, then arrange on a plate. Melt the butter in a small pan, add the lemon zest and juice, turn up the heat, stir in the Parmesan—the sauce will begin to thicken slightly—then pour it over the asparagus.

Lift out the poached eggs with a slotted spoon, dry on a dish towel, and place on top of the asparagus. Sprinkle with a little Parmesan, lemon zest, and freshly ground black pepper. Serve immediately with lots of good bread to mop up the sauce.

SCAPECE DI ZUCCHINI AL LIMONE

Lemon-marinated zucchini

This traditional Neapolitan dish was originally made as a way of preserving zucchini when they were in season, but wine vinegar was always used. The dish is still made with vinegar today and usually served with a selection of antipasti. Lemon juice preserves just as well and is ideal for anyone who dislikes the strong taste of vinegar. Perfect served as part of an antipasto or as an accompaniment to fish dishes like the sole *involtini* on page 104.

Serves 4
vegetable oil, for frying
12 oz (350 g) zucchini, washed,
    dried, and thinly sliced into rounds
1 garlic clove, very finely chopped
10 mint leaves, finely chopped
zest of 1 unwaxed lemon and 4 tsp lemon juice
sea salt

Pour vegetable oil into a frying pan to a depth of about ½ inch (1 cm) and place over the heat. When it is hot, drop in the zucchini slices and fry for 3–4 minutes until golden. Drain on paper towels, then place in a bowl with a sprinkling of salt, garlic, mint leaves, and lemon juice. Toss together and leave to rest for at least 20 minutes. Sprinkle with some freshly grated lemon zest before serving.

FIORI DI ZUCCHINE RIPIENI

Filled zucchini flowers

This has got to be one of the nicest ways of enjoying vegetables, not only pretty to look at but delicious—once you start eating them, you will wish you made more! I am always so surprised when people get rid of zucchni flowers. They are so popular in Italy and we use them in all sorts of recipes. Zucchini flowers are available during spring and summer so look out for them at the market or greengrocer or perhaps you grow your own. You may find you need more or less zucchini flowers depending on their size.

Serves 4
8 zucchini flowers
vegetable oil for deep-frying
lemon zest, to serve

For the filling
1 cup (250 g) ricotta
⅓ cup (30 g) grated Parmesan cheese
juice of 1 small lemon
½ cup (30 g) dried breadcrumbs
½ handful of basil leaves, finely chopped
sea salt and freshly ground black pepper

For the batter
3 eggs, separated
2 tsp lemon juice
3 tbsp all-purpose flour
sea salt

First make the filling by combining all the ingredients. Place the mixture into a pastry bag if you have one and set aside.

Carefully open up the zucchini flowers from the tip, remove any stamens, and fill each one with the ricotta mixture. Close the flower by gently twisting the end of the petals to seal.

Beat the egg yolks until nice and creamy. In another clean bowl, whisk the egg whites with the lemon juice and a pinch of salt until stiff, then gently fold into the egg yolks and fold in the all-purpose flour.

continued on next page...

In the meantime, heat plenty of oil in a large pot to deep-fry the flowers. Holding them by the stem, dip the filled flowers one by one into the egg mixture, gently coating them completely. Place in the hot oil and fry for 3 or 4 minutes until golden-brown. Turn during frying so they have an even golden color.

Remove, drain on paper towels, and serve immediately with a sprinkle of freshly grated lemon zest. Delicious enjoyed with a drizzle of lemon juice.

FISH

SPAGHETTI CON ACCIUGHE E NOCI AL PROFUMO DI LIMONE

Spaghetti with anchovies, walnuts, and lemon juice

It's quite common to serve pasta with anchovies and walnuts, especially in southern Italy, when the fridge is bare and you need to prepare something quick and easy. I have elaborated it here with the addition of capers, parsley, and tomatoes—that's what I had on hand when testing this recipe! The addition of lemon juice really gives a tangy zing to the dish and I love to add more when eating.

Serves 2
7 oz (200 g) spaghetti
3 tablespoons extra virgin olive oil
1 garlic clove, finely sliced
15 capers
12 anchovy fillets, rinsed if salted
5 sweet baby plum tomatoes, halved
2 tbsp grated Parmesan cheese, plus extra to serve
juice of ½ lemon, plus extra to serve
handful of flat-leaf parsley, roughly chopped
pat of butter
¼ cup (30 g) roughly chopped walnuts
sea salt and freshly ground black pepper

Bring a large saucepan of salted water to a boil, add the spaghetti, and cook until al dente.

Meanwhile, heat the extra virgin olive oil in a frying pan, add the garlic and capers, and sweat for a minute or so over medium heat. Add the anchovy fillets and, mixing with a wooden spoon, cook until dissolved. Stir in the tomatoes and about 6 tablespoons of the hot pasta cooking water and cook over medium heat for 5 minutes.

Drain the pasta and, using a pair of tongs, add it to the pan, mixing everything together over the heat. Stir in the Parmesan, lemon juice, parsley, butter, and a grind of black pepper. Mix well. Serve immediately, sprinkled with the chopped walnuts, some extra Parmesan, and a squeeze of lemon.

L'INSALATA DI MERLUZZO DI MAMMA

My mom's cod salad

This was my mom's recipe, which she would often cook for my sister and me. The addition of cooking water was to make the dish go further by dipping bread into the sauce and mopping up all the juices. It was, and still is, one of my favorite ways to enjoy fish—it's simple, delicious, and reminds me of my mamma. For Christmas Eve, we would have a similar salad made with *baccala* (salted cod), which is traditionally eaten during the festive season. This dish makes a lovely sharing platter as an antipasto or can be enjoyed as a light main course with lots of good bread.

Serves 4–6
1¼ lb (550 g) cod fillet
4 tbsp extra virgin olive oil
2 tbsp lemon juice
1 garlic clove, finely sliced
a small handful of flat-leaf parsley leaves, finely chopped
8 pitted green olives, halved or sliced
a little red chili pepper, finely chopped (optional)
sea salt

Poach the fish in slightly salted water for about 5 minutes or so until cooked through. Drain, but reserve some of the cooking water. Place the cooked cod on a serving dish or divide among plates.

Combine the extra virgin olive oil, lemon juice, garlic, some salt, parsley, and 3 tablespoons of the cooking water. Whisk well together and pour over the fish. Top with the green olives and sprinkle with a little red chili pepper, if desired. Serve with lots of good bread to mop up the dressing.

LINGUINE CON PESTO AL PISTACCHIO E TONNO

Linguine with pistachio pesto and tuna

This simple pasta dish is a complete meal. The tangy lemon flavor gives a lovely kick to canned tuna. It's worth making more pesto than the amount you need for this recipe; covered, it keeps for about three days in the fridge and you can serve it with pasta on another occasion or use it to top crostini.

Serves 4
11½ oz (320 g) linguine
4 tbsp extra virgin olive oil
2 garlic cloves, finely chopped
3–4 cans tuna, drained (drained weight approx. 11½ oz/320 g)
zest of 1 unwaxed lemon and a squeeze of juice
sea salt and freshly ground black pepper

For the pesto
⅔ cup (200 g) unsalted pistachio nuts
⅓ cup (30 g) grated Parmesan cheese
zest of 1 unwaxed lemon
5 basil leaves
½ garlic clove
⅔ cup (160 ml) extra virgin olive oil
generous ½ cup (140 ml) warm water

First make the pesto. Put all the ingredients into a blender and blend to a smooth consistency. Set aside.

Bring a large pot of salted water to a boil and cook the linguine until al dente.

Meanwhile, heat the extra virgin olive oil in a large frying pan, add the garlic, and sweat over medium heat for a minute. Add the tuna chunks and a little salt and pepper to taste, and cook for a minute or so to allow the flavors to infuse. Drain the linguine, mix with the pesto and tuna, and stir well together. Sprinkle with lemon zest and a squeeze of lemon and serve immediately.

RISOTTO AI GAMBERI E LIMONE

Shrimp and lemon risotto

Lovely creamy, lemony risotto with jumbo shrimp is a match made in heaven! This is delicate, light, and a perfect meal at any time. Try to get the freshest shrimp you can for maximum flavor.

Serves 2
2 tbsp extra virgin olive oil
1 banana shallot, finely chopped
8 raw jumbo shrimp, peeled and roughly chopped
¾ cup (140 g) risotto rice (carnaroli, vialone nano, or arborio)
3 tbsp lemon juice, plus extra for drizzling
3 cups (700 ml) hot vegetable stock (you may need a little extra)
1½ tbsp (20 g) butter
zest of ½ unwaxed lemon
a small handful of flat-leaf parsley leaves, finely chopped

Heat the extra virgin olive oil in a pan, add the shallot and shrimp, and sweat over medium heat for a couple of minutes until the shallot has softened and the shrimp has colored slightly. Add the rice and stir with a wooden spoon until each grain is coated in the oil. Stir in the lemon juice and cook, stirring continuously, until the liquid is almost all absorbed. Add a ladleful of hot stock, stirring until absorbed, and continue adding and stirring for 15–17 minutes until the rice is cooked—it should be soft on the outside but al dente on the inside.

Remove from the heat, beat in the butter, stir in the lemon zest and parsley, and serve immediately with a drizzle of lemon juice if desired.

BRANZINO ALL'ACQUA PAZZA AL LIMONE CON VERDURINE

Seabass fillets in lemon "crazy water" with vegetables

I dedicate this dish to my friends at Giardiniello restaurant in Minori, who cook fillets of white fish in this way using olive oil, lemon juice, and water. The term "crazy water" is often given to southern Italian fish dishes cooked in water, such as this one. This recipe is simple and very quick to prepare, but you can also get it wrong. The secret to this dish is to keep the pan moving, but not stir the veggies or fish. If easier, lift the pan slightly off the burner, so it is still touching the gas flame, and keep moving it—this way the veggies and fish will cook through delicately as well as imparting the lemon flavor, and the liquid will thicken very slightly. Serve with good bread to mop up the delicious sauce.

Serves 2

2 seabass fillets (approx. 6¼ oz/180 g total weight)
6 tbsp extra virgin olive oil
⅓ cup (80 ml) lemon juice
½ celery stick, cut into thin matchsticks
½ carrot, cut into thin matchsticks
½ zucchini, firm part with skin only, cut into matchsticks
¼ red onion, thinly sliced
sea salt and black pepper
a couple of flat-leaf parsley sprigs, to garnish (optional)

Slice the seabass fillets in half and set aside.

Put the extra virgin olive oil, lemon juice, and a little salt and pepper in a frying pan over medium heat. Add all the vegetables and cook over medium heat for a couple of minutes, shaking the pan from time to time. Remove the vegetables with a slotted spoon and arrange on a serving dish.

Put the pan back on the heat and add 8 tablespoons of water. Place the fish fillets in the pan and cook on each side for a couple of minutes, shaking the pan but being careful not to break the fish. Carefully remove the fish and arrange over the vegetables on the serving platter.

Place the pan with its cooking liquid back on the heat, shaking it for a few seconds, then pour the sauce over the fish and vegetables and serve immediately, garnished with a couple parsley sprigs, if desired.

ORATA AL LIMONE AL CARTOCCIO
Steam-baked lemon-infused seabream

I love cooking fish *al cartoccio* (steam-baked), which is not only a healthy way of cooking, but the parcel seals in all the flavors (and saves on washing up!). Ask your fishmonger to clean the seabream and make a slit down its belly so you can fill the cavity. The subtle lemon flavor really comes out and for an added kick, I like to serve this dish with Sicilian Dressing (page 184).

Serves 2
1 whole seabream, weighing approx. 1 lb (450 g)
1 garlic clove, finely chopped
handful of flat-leaf parsley, roughly chopped, plus extra sprigs
leaves of 2 thyme sprigs, plus an extra sprig
¼ red chili pepper, finely chopped
1 tbsp extra virgin olive oil, plus extra for drizzling
zest and juice of ½ unwaxed lemon
3 lemon slices, halved (depending on the size; if using
    small lemons, keep the slices whole)
Sicilian Dressing (page 184), optional
sea salt

Preheat the oven to 350°F (180°C).

Rinse the seabream under cold running water, then pat dry with paper towels or a dish towel. Stack a large piece of parchment paper over a large piece of aluminum foil and place the fish in the center.

Combine the garlic, parsley, thyme leaves, chili, extra virgin olive oil, and lemon zest and juice and fill the cavity of the seabream with this mixture, followed by a couple of the lemon slices. Sprinkle the fish all over with salt, place the remaining lemon slices on top with the parsley and thyme sprigs, and drizzle all over with extra virgin olive oil. Then wrap tightly in the foil, place on a flat baking pan, and bake in the oven for 40 minutes.

Remove from the oven, carefully unwrap the parcel, and serve the fish with Sicilian Dressing (page 184) if desired.

MERLUZZO CON CROSTA DI ERBE MISTE E LIMONE

Cod fillets with a mixed herb and lemon crust

This delicious and simple fish dish is quick and easy to prepare and makes a lovely meal for any day of the week. The lemon juice enhances the breadcrumb coating and complements the fish fillets perfectly. I have used cod, but hake is just as good. Serve with some boiled new potatoes and a green salad.

Serves 4
4 cod fillets, weighing approx. 7 oz (200 g) each
extra virgin olive oil
lemon wedges, to serve

For the crust
3½ oz (100 g) bread (crusts removed)
2 small thyme sprigs, leaves stripped
a small handful of flat-leaf parsley
1 rosemary sprig, needles stripped
scant 2 tbsp capers
1 garlic clove
2 anchovy fillets
juice of ½ lemon
1 tbsp extra virgin olive oil
sea salt and freshly ground black pepper

Preheat the oven to 425°F (220°C).

Place all the crust ingredients in a blender and blend until fairly smooth. Set aside.

Pat dry the fish fillets using paper towels to ensure there is no moisture. Rub a little salt and pepper all over the fillets, then a little extra virgin olive oil.

Heat a nonstick frying pan, preferably ovenproof, over medium heat. Place the fish in the pan skin-side down and fry for a minute or so, then turn over carefully and fry for another couple of minutes on the other side. Remove from the heat—if your pan is not ovenproof, carefully transfer the fish into an ovenproof dish. Top each fillet with the breadcrumb mixture and place in the hot oven for 8 minutes until the crust is golden. Remove from the oven and serve immediately with lemon wedges.

INVOLTINI DI SOGLIOLA AL FORNO

Baked rolled sole fillets

Sole is a delicately flavored fish, which is perfectly enhanced with this subtle paste of capers, anchovies, parsley, and lemon. Make sure you cover the dish with foil for the first 10 minutes so the fish inside can steam nicely. Serve 2 *involtini* per person, accompanied by Sautéed Green Beans (page 74) or Marinated Zucchini (page 84) or a simple green salad for a lovely, light, and healthy main course.

Serves 2

2 sole fillets, weighing approx. 5½ oz (150 g) each
breadcrumbs, for sprinkling
extra virgin olive oil
4 large bay leaves
4 slices of lemon
sea salt and freshly ground black pepper

For the filling

scant 2 tbsp capers, finely chopped
3 anchovy fillets, finely chopped
½ garlic clove, finely chopped
zest of ½ unwaxed lemon
½ handful of flat-leaf parsley leaves, finely chopped
2 tsp extra virgin olive oil

Preheat the oven to 350°F (180°C).

Cut the sole fillets in half lengthways so you end up with four long pieces. Place skin-side down with the widest part nearest to you.

Combine all the filling ingredients and spread over the sole fillets, sprinkle some breadcrumbs over, and carefully roll them up starting with the wider part.

Drizzle the base of an oven dish with a little extra virgin olive oil, then arrange the bay leaves in the dish and top each leaf with a lemon slice. Place a sole *involtino* over each lemon slice, seam-side down. Sprinkle the fish with salt and pepper and drizzle with extra virgin olive oil.

Cover with foil and bake in the oven for 20 minutes, removing the foil halfway through. Remove from the oven and serve immediately.

SARDINE RIPIENE

Filled sardines coated in breadcrumbs

This recipe is inspired by a similar one made by the chef of my favorite restaurant, Giardiniello, in Minori, who uses anchovies freshly caught off the Amalfi coast and fills with them with the local provola cheese. Since fresh anchovies are not readily available everywhere, I decided to use sardines and fill them with a tuna and lemon filling. If you are able to get fresh anchovies, by all means use them, but since they are smaller you will probably need to use two anchovies at a time and sandwich them together with the filling. If you can't get either fish or just like the taste of the filling, you can make the filling mixture into delicious *polpettine* (see page 42).

Serves 4
3 eggs, beaten with a little salt
breadcrumbs, for coating
12 headless sardines, cleaned and butterflied
vegetable or sunflower oil, for shallow frying
lemon wedges, to serve

For the filling
¾ cup (120 g) canned tuna (drained weight)
¼ cup (60 g) ricotta cheese
2 tsp finely chopped flat-leaf parsley
2 anchovy fillets, finely chopped
heaped 1 tbsp capers, finely chopped
2 tbsp grated Parmesan cheese
zest of 1 unwaxed lemon
5 tsp lemon juice

First make the filling. Combine all the ingredients to make a smooth, but not runny mixture and set aside.

Prepare two bowls, one with the beaten eggs and the other with lots of breadcrumbs and set aside.

Pat dry the sardines with paper towels and lay them flat on a board or work surface, skin-side down. Place some filling in each cavity and close the sardine—don't worry if the filling is showing as it will be covered by breadcrumbs. Dip the filled sardines in beaten egg then coat well in breadcrumbs.

Heat enough oil to cover the base of a large frying pan; when hot lower in the sardines, filling-side down, and fry for a minute or so. Then turn over with the aid of a pair of tongs and continue to fry until golden all over. Remove from the heat and drain on paper towels. Serve immediately with lemon wedges.

TRANCI DI SALMONE AL FORNO CON FINOCCHIO E AGRUMI

Baked salmon steaks with fennel, orange, and lemon

Fish, fennel, and citrus fruits go so well together. This delicate salmon dish is simple to prepare and makes a tasty meal perhaps served with a green salad. Salmon steaks are quite large so it's up to you whether you want to serve a whole one per person or share it between two. If you prefer, you could make this with salmon fillets and if so, reduce the cooking time by about 7–10 minutes.

Serves 2–4
1 fennel bulb, sliced, green fronds reserved
a little extra virgin olive oil
6 thin lemon slices
6 thin orange slices
2 large salmon steaks weighing approx. 10½ oz (300 g) each
squeeze of lemon juice
a few flat-leaf parsley leaves
breadcrumbs, for sprinkling
sea salt and freshly ground black pepper

Preheat the oven to 350°F (180°C).

Put the fennel slices in a pan of boiling water and blanch for a couple of minutes. Drain well and set aside.

Lightly grease an ovenproof dish with a little extra virgin olive oil, then line with the lemon and orange slices. Place the salmon steaks on top, sprinkle with salt and pepper, drizzle with a little lemon juice, scatter over some parsley, top with the green fennel fronds and fennel slices, and another sprinkle of salt and pepper. Sprinkle the breadcrumbs all over and bake in the oven for about 25 minutes until the fish is cooked through.

Remove from the oven and serve immediately.

MERLUZZO AL BURRO E LIMONE

Hake with butter and lemon

The combination of butter, lemon, and capers with white fish is perfect. Very simple and quick to prepare, this light fish dish can be served with some boiled baby potatoes and Sautéed Green Beans (page 74). If you prefer you can use cod, fillets of seabass or seabream, or other white fish.

Serves 4
4 hake fillets (approx. 1 lb 5 oz/600 g total weight)
7 tbsp (100 g) butter
3 anchovy fillets, finely chopped
2 tbsp capers
zest of ½ unwaxed lemon and 4 tbsp juice
8 mint leaves, finely chopped
sea salt and freshly ground black pepper

Season the hake all over with salt and pepper.

Melt 3 tablespoons (40 g) of the butter in a large frying pan over medium heat, add the anchovy fillets, and cook for a minute or so until they dissolve. Add the hake fillets and cook for a couple of minutes on each side, then place skin-side down. Add the capers, half the lemon juice, 2 tablespoons (30 g) of the butter, and half the mint and continue to cook for 2–3 minutes until the hake is cooked through.

Transfer the hake to a serving dish, add the remaining butter to the pan, increase the heat, stir in the remaining lemon juice, and pour over the fish. Sprinkle with the lemon zest and remaining mint and serve immediately.

MEAT

PICCATINA AL LIMONE
Veal escalopes with butter and lemon

This classic meat dish has always been a favorite on Italian menus the world over. It can also be made with pork or chicken escalopes. Serve with boiled baby potatoes and lemony carrots for a quick and delicious meal.

Serves 4
14 oz (400 g) veal escalopes, thinly sliced
all-purpose flour, for dusting
5½ tbsp (80 g) butter
5 sage leaves
zest and juice of 1 unwaxed lemon
⅓ cup (80 ml) white wine
sea salt and freshly ground black pepper
lemon wedges, to serve

For the carrots
8 medium carrots
2 tbsp extra virgin olive oil
Juice of ½ lemon
½ handful of flat-leaf parsley, roughly chopped

Dust the meat in flour, shaking off the excess.

Cook the carrots in boiling water until nearly tender, about 15 minutes. Drain and place the carrots in a frying pan with the olive oil and saute for about 4 minutes. Add the lemon juice and parsley and keep warm to serve with the veal.

Melt the butter in a large frying pan and add the sage leaves. Add the veal slices and fry over medium heat for about 3 minutes on each side.

Pour in the lemon juice and white wine and, shaking the pan, allow to evaporate gently until the sauce has reduced by half and has a creamy consistency. Remove from the heat, season with salt and pepper to taste, and serve immediately with lemon zest and lemon wedges.

INVOLTINI DI POLLO ALLA SICILIANA

Sicilian-style chicken involtini

These delicious chicken rolls are filled with typically Sicilian ingredients of pistachios and citrus fruits. The addition of salami gives the filling an extra kick—try to get a whole piece of salami as opposed to slices, so you can cut it into small cubes. I suggest a plain pork salami, such as Milano or Napoli. If you prefer, you could substitute the chicken with pork or veal escalopes, pounding them well to get thin slices.

Serves 4 (makes approx. 8)
1 lb 2 oz (500 g) chicken breast, sliced horizontally
    into about 8 thin escalopes
extra virgin olive oil
breadcrumbs, for sprinkling
sea salt and freshly ground black pepper

For the filling
3½ oz (100 g) bread, crusts removed
⅓ cup (30 g) grated Parmesan cheese
2½ tbsp pistachios, finely chopped
2¼ oz (65 g) salami, chopped into small cubes
zest and juice of ½ unwaxed orange
zest and juice of ½ unwaxed lemon

Preheat the oven to 350°F (180°C) and lightly grease a baking pan.

Place the chicken breasts on a large board or work surface, sprinkle with a little salt and pepper, and rub extra virgin olive oil all over them.

Combine all the filling ingredients, including some black pepper and enough extra virgin olive oil to make the filling stick together—a bit like dough. Divide the filling into eight pieces, form into small sausage shapes, then place on the chicken and roll up to enclose the filling. Secure with toothpicks or wooden skewers.

Place the *involtini* on the baking pan, sprinkle with breadcrumbs, drizzle with extra virgin olive oil, and bake in the oven for 25 minutes. Insert the tip of a sharp knife to check that the chicken is cooked through. Remove from the oven and serve immediately.

POLLO ARROSTO CON ERBE AL PROFUMO DI LIMONE

Lemon and herb-infused roast chicken with lemon gravy

I always like to add a buttery paste on the chicken flesh underneath the skin to add flavor and keep it nice and moist during cooking. You can use this same recipe to liven up roast turkey, capon, and guinea fowl. The lemon and herb flavors really come through, making this a tasty Sunday lunch. When making the gravy with the roasting juices, I like to add lemon juice for an extra lemony hit. The flavor is not overpowering; in fact lemon combines so well with the herbs and juices from the roast chicken, you will always want to cook roast chicken this way! Serve with roast potatoes.

Serves 4
3½ lb (1.6 kg) free-range organic chicken
handful of mixed fresh herbs—rosemary sprigs, thyme sprigs,
    bay leaves, and sage leaves—tied in a bunch
2 large carrots, halved lengthways
2 large leeks, halved lengthways
extra virgin olive oil, for drizzling
scant 1 cup (200 ml) white wine
1 tsp water
juice of ½ lemon
2 tsp all-purpose flour
sea salt and freshly ground black pepper

For the lemon & herb butter
11 tbsp (150 g) butter, softened at room temperature
needles from 2 rosemary sprigs, finely chopped
leaves from 4 thyme sprigs
6 sage leaves, finely chopped
1 garlic clove, finely chopped
zest of 2 unwaxed lemons and juice of 1 lemon—
    reserve two of the lemon halves

Preheat the oven to 425°F (220°C).

Combine all the ingredients for the herb butter until you obtain a smooth paste.

continued on next page...

Take the chicken and, starting at the neck end, gently ease the skin of the chicken away from the breast, taking care not to tear the delicate skin. Using your fingers, spread three-quarters of the paste as evenly as possible under the skin all over the breast and thighs, then gently pat the skin to even out the paste. Then fill the chicken cavity with the two reserved lemon halves and bunch of mixed herbs.

Line a roasting pan with the carrots and leeks and drizzle with a little extra virgin olive oil. Place the chicken on top of the vegetables—this will prevent the chicken from sticking to the pan. Season the chicken all over with salt and pepper, drizzle with a little extra virgin olive oil, and rub well all over. Pour in the wine and water and cover with foil.

Reduce the oven temperature to 400°F (200°C) and roast the chicken for 1 hour 30–1 hour 40 minutes removing the foil for the last 30 minutes, until cooked through. During cooking, baste the chicken with the juices from time to time.

Remove the roasting pan from the oven and immediately place the remaining butter paste on top of the chicken to melt, using a spatula to spread it all over. Carefully transfer the chicken and vegetables to a board and leave to rest for about 10 minutes before carving.

In the meantime, make the gravy. Combine the juices left in the roasting pan with the lemon juice and a scant 1 cup (200 ml) of water and place over high heat (transfer to a frying pan if you need to). Whisk in the flour and continue mixing until the gravy has thickened slightly. Strain, pour the gravy into a jug, and serve with the roast chicken and vegetables.

CONIGLIO AL FORNO DI ERMINIA CON LE FOGLIE DI LIMONE

Erminia's recipe for rabbit baked in lemon leaves

This traditional recipe is from the village of Conca dei Marini on the Amalfi coast. It was given to my sister Adriana by her friend Erminia, who originates from the village. An abundance of fresh lemon leaves is used to slow-roast chunks of rabbit that have been coated in a delicious breadcrumb mixture. The delicate rabbit meat is subtly flavored by the essential oil exuded from the lemon leaves during cooking. If you are unable to get lemon leaves, you can still make this recipe using lemon slices. Either way, it's delicious served with Lemon Salsa Verde (page 185) or Lemon Mayo (page 182) and a mixed salad.

Serves 4–6
2¾ lb (1.2 kg) rabbit, deboned and cut into chunks
zest and juice of 1 unwaxed lemon
approx. 1¾ cups (100 g) dried breadcrumbs
½ cup (50 g) grated pecorino cheese
a small handful of flat-leaf parsley leaves, finely chopped
1 rosemary sprig, needles stripped and finely chopped
1 large garlic clove, very finely chopped
extra virgin olive oil
vegetable or sunflower oil, for greasing
abundant fresh lemon leaves, or
   2 lemons, thinly sliced
sea salt

Rinse the rabbit under cold running water and pat dry on paper towels. Place in a large bowl, drizzle with the lemon juice, and top with enough cold water to cover the meat. Cover and set aside for a couple of hours—in hot weather, refrigerate.

Combine the breadcrumbs, pecorino, parsley, rosemary, garlic, and lemon zest.

Preheat the oven to 375°F (190°C). Drain the rabbit well and rub salt and extra virgin olive oil all over each piece, then coat in the breadcrumb mixture.

Grease a large roasting pan with some oil and line the base with about one-third of the lemon leaves or half of the lemon slices, slightly overlapping them so that the base is covered. Place the rabbit chunks on top, cover with another third of the lemon leaves or the rest of the slices, and drizzle with some oil.

continued on next page...

Roast in the oven for 90 minutes. Halfway through the cooking time, remove the pan, turn the rabbit chunks over, then place the remaining lemon leaves over the top (if using). At the end of cooking time, increase the heat to 400°F (200°C), discard the top leaves, and continue to cook for about 5 minutes until the rabbit is golden. Remove from the oven and serve.

AGNELLO PASQUALE CON UOVA E LIMONE

Easter lamb with eggs and lemon

This traditional lamb dish is popular in central and southern Italy during the spring, especially around Easter when lamb is at its best and eggs are celebrated. The tangy taste of lemon gives a kick to the lamb, balancing its often strong flavor. Serve with good bread to mop up the sauce and Sautéed Green Beans (page 74) or a green salad.

Serves 4

3 tbsp extra virgin olive oil
1 onion, finely sliced
1 garlic clove, finely chopped
1 rosemary sprig, plus ½ sprig, needles stripped
    and finely chopped
2¼ lb (1 kg) lamb shoulder, deboned and cut into chunks
    (about 1 lb 10 oz/750 g prepared)
juice and zest of 2 unwaxed lemons
⅔ cup (150 ml) vegetable stock
2 eggs
scant ½ cup (40 g) grated pecorino cheese
sea salt and freshly ground black pepper

Heat the extra virgin olive oil in a large pot, add the onion, and sweat over medium heat for 2–3 minutes until softened. Add the garlic and the whole rosemary sprig and continue to cook for a minute. Add the lamb, increase the heat, and sear well on all sides. Pour in the lemon juice and stock, reduce the heat, cover with a lid, and cook gently for 1½ hours until the lamb is tender.

Near the end of the cooking time, combine the eggs, pecorino, chopped rosemary, lemon zest, and some salt and pepper.

Remove the pan from the heat and very gradually stir in the egg mixture until you obtain a creamy sauce, making sure the eggs don't scramble. Serve immediately.

Tip
If you plan to serve this later, add the egg mixture just before serving.

LEPRE AL LIMONE CON PATATE E MELE

Lemon-infused hare with potatoes and apples

Lemon and apple lend a lovely sweet and sour flavor to hare, which is a meat I love. We would often have hare in Italy and it was always soaked in water and lemon juice to remove any impurities and reduce its strong gamey flavor. If you prefer, you can make this rustic dish using rabbit or chicken instead.

Serves 4–6
2¾ lb (1.2 kg) prepared hare, on the bone
   but cut into chunks
zest and juice of 1 unwaxed lemon, the two halves reserved
3 apples, cored and sliced into thick rings
½ cup (120 ml) lemon juice (from about 2 large lemons),
   plus extra for drizzling
4 tbsp extra virgin olive oil
3 rosemary sprigs
scant ½ cup (100 ml) white wine
3½ cups (800 ml) vegetable stock
1 lb 10 oz (750 g) potatoes, peeled and cut into chunks
4 tbsp (60 g) butter
sea salt and freshly ground black pepper

Place the hare chunks in a bowl, cover with cold water, add the juice of 1 lemon plus the squeezed lemon halves, and leave to soak for about 20 minutes.

Drizzle the apple rings with ½ cup (120 ml) of lemon juice, set aside.

Drain the hare chunks, pat dry with paper towels, and season all over with salt and pepper.

Heat the extra virgin olive oil in a large pot, add the rosemary, and sweat for a minute over medium heat. Add the hare chunks and sear well on all sides. Drain the lemon juice from the apples (set them aside) and add it to the pan with the white wine. Allow to evaporate slightly. Add the stock, bring to a boil, then reduce the heat, cover with a lid, and cook for about 50 minutes until the meat is tender. About halfway through, add the potatoes.

Towards the end of cooking time, melt the butter in a frying pan, add the apple rings, and caramelize them on both sides. Place on a large serving dish with the hare and potatoes and sprinkle with the lemon zest. Serve immediately with a drizzle of lemon juice, if desired.

ARROSTO DI MAIALE AL LIMONE SERVITO CON SPINACI

Rolled roast pork loin served with spinach

This dish makes a great light Sunday lunch. Ask your butcher to butterfly the pork loin for you to make it easier and quicker to prepare. I have used cipolotti, which are fat scallions but you can equally use regular ones. The pork can be eaten hot or cold—in fact it's more delicious the following day once all the flavors have infused, enhancing the lemon and rosemary taste.

Serves 6
pared rind of 2 unwaxed lemons
1 tsp sugar
2 tbsp extra virgin olive oil, plus extra for drizzling
6 rosemary sprigs
9 oz (250 g) cipolotti onions (or scallions, white and green parts), trimmed
2¼ lb (1 kg) pork loin, cut into a long piece ready for rolling
⅔ cup (150 ml) white wine
sea salt and freshly ground black pepper

For the spinach
2 tbsp extra virgin olive oil
4 whole, unpeeled garlic cloves
7 oz (200 g) baby spinach
juice of 1 lemon
sea salt

Preheat the oven to 400°F (200°C).

In a small saucepan, combine the lemon rind with the sugar and enough water to cover. Bring to a boil and boil for 10 minutes. Drain the water, pat the rind dry, and set it aside.

Heat 2 tablespoons of extra virgin olive oil in a frying pan large enough to accommodate the pork loin. Add the rosemary and cipolotti and gently fry, stirring, for about 7 minutes (less if you are using regular scallions) until golden and slightly softened. Remove from the heat and set aside.

continued on next page...

Unroll the pork loin and place it on a flat surface skin side down, flattening it slightly with a meat tenderizer. Drizzle with a little extra virgin olive oil, sprinkle with salt, pepper, and the needles from 2 of the rosemary sprigs. Slice the cipolotti in two lengthways (if using scallions keep them whole) and set one-quarter of them aside. Place the rest of the onions or scallions on the pork loin, together with three-quarters of the lemon peel. Roll the pork up and tie tightly with kitchen string.

Return the frying pan to the heat (it will still contain olive oil and the remaining rosemary). Sear the pork on all sides. Pour in the white wine and allow to evaporate slightly. Remove from the heat.

Drizzle a little extra virgin olive oil into a roasting pan, place the reserved cipolotti or scallions on the bottom of the roasting pan with the remaining rosemary sprigs. Place the pork on top, drizzle with a little extra virgin olive oil, pour over the juices from the frying pan, and cover with foil. Roast in the oven for about 1 hour, basting from time to time. If necessary, add a little hot water to the roasting pan during cooking to prevent it from drying out. Remove the foil for the last 15 minutes.

Remove from the oven, leave to rest for 5–10 minutes, pour the juices into a jug, and keep warm.

Meanwhile, prepare the spinach. Heat the extra virgin olive oil in a frying pan, add the garlic cloves, and sweat over medium heat for 3 minutes. Add the spinach, a little salt, and cook, stirring, for a couple of minutes until wilted. Remove from the pan and drizzle with lemon juice.

Slice the pork, garnish with the remaining lemon rind, and serve with the juices and spinach.

BURGER DI TACCHINO AL PROFUMO DI LIMONE

Lemon-infused turkey burgers

For a lighter, healthier burger than the usual beef, try these ground turkey burgers with a delicious hint of herbs and lemon. Enjoy them by themselves accompanied with Roasted Pepper Salad (page 45) or in a bun with some Lemon Mayo (page 182).

Makes 6

1¾ oz (50 g) stale bread, soaked in a little warm water
14 oz (400 g) ground turkey
2 garlic cloves, finely chopped
1 rosemary sprig, needles stripped and finely chopped
2 thyme sprigs, leaves stripped and finely chopped
⅓ cup (30 g) grated Parmesan cheese
zest and juice of 1 unwaxed lemon
1 egg
all-purpose flour, for dusting
2–3 tbsp extra virgin olive oil
4 tbsp water
sea salt and freshly ground black pepper

To serve (optional)
Roasted Pepper Salad (page 45)
6 burger buns
Lemon Mayo (page 182)
large handful of arugula leaves
parmesan shavings
grated lemon zest

Remove the bread from the water, use your hands to squeeze out the excess liquid, then finely chop.

In a bowl, combine the ground turkey, bread, garlic, herbs, Parmesan, lemon zest, egg, and some salt and pepper. Divide the mixture into six pieces, shape into burger patties, and lightly dust with flour.

Heat the olive oil in a large frying pan and fry the burgers over high heat for 2–3 minutes on each side until golden and a slight crust has formed. Combine the lemon juice and measured water and pour over the burgers. Cover with a lid, reduce the heat to medium, and cook for about 2 minutes until the liquid has been absorbed. Remove from the heat and serve with a sprinkle of lemon zest and roasted red pepper salad, or in a bun with some lemon mayo, arugula, parmesan, and freshly grated lemon zest.

DESSERTS

SORBETTO AL LIMONE E MENTA

Lemon and mint sorbet

This tangy refreshing sorbet is perfect on hot summer days but it's just as enjoyable during winter. Serve with mixed berries for a refreshing dessert and some Lemon Cookies (page 136).

Serves 4–6
4 unwaxed lemons
approx. 30 mint leaves
1⅓ cups (250 g) sugar
Generous 2 cups (500 ml) water

Finely pare the rind from 2 of the lemons, trying to avoid the white pith as much as possible, and grate the other 2 using a zester. Then halve and juice all 4 lemons. Finely chop half of the mint leaves.

Place the lemon rind, sugar, water, and whole mint leaves in a saucepan and bring to a boil, stirring from time to time. Continue to boil for 7 minutes then remove from the heat and allow to cool.

When cool, discard the rind (or reserve for decoration) and mint leaves. Combine the liquid with the lemon zest and finely chopped mint. Pour into a lidded freezerproof container and place in the freezer for 4–5 hours. Every hour or so, give the sorbet a good stir with a small whisk to break up the ice crystals.

Remove from the freezer and leave at room temperature for about 20 minutes before serving. Decorate with the lemon rind and extra fresh mint leaves if desired.

BISCOTTI MORBIDI AL LIMONE
Lemon cookies

These deliciously soft cookies with an aromatic hint of lemon are really addictive. When we tested them for this book, we began eating them straight from the oven and their lovely aroma filled the house. If you can resist them for longer, they will keep for about a week in an airtight container. You can also make them with orange or combine both for a delicious citrussy flavor.

Makes approx. 25
7 tbsp (100 g) butter, softened at room temperature
scant ½ cup (80 g) sugar, plus extra for coating
1 egg, lightly beaten
zest and juice of 1 unwaxed lemon
2½ cups (300 g) self-rising flour, sifted
Confectioner's sugar, sifted, for coating

Line a large cookie sheet with parchment paper.

In a large bowl, beat the butter and sugar until creamy, then gradually beat in the egg and combine well. Stir in the lemon zest and juice and gradually add the flour until it is all incorporated, forming a soft dough. Shape into a ball, wrap in plastic, and leave to rest in the fridge for 1 hour.

Meanwhile, preheat the oven to 350°F (180°C).

Take two plates and scatter granulated sugar on one and sifted confectioner's sugar on the other.

Remove the cookie dough from the fridge and remove the plastic. Using your hands pull off walnut-size pieces of dough and form into balls. Roll first in the granulated sugar and then in confectioner's sugar, coating well all over. Place on the prepared baking pan (no need to flatten them).

Bake in the oven for about 12 minutes until they are just beginning to turn slightly golden and cracks form on the top. Remove from the oven and enjoy!

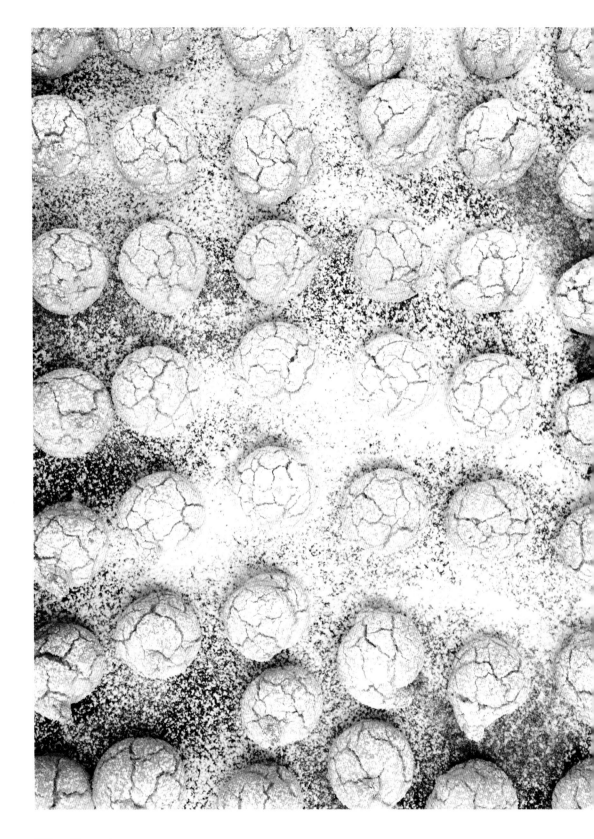

TORTA DELIZIA AL LIMONE

Creamy lemon cake

This cake is a twist on the classic Delizia al Limone, the individual dome-shaped sponge cakes filled and covered with lemon cream that are so popular in pastry shops along the Amalfi coast. It's really quite simple to make yet it looks really impactful—perfect for a special occasion. For flavor, I use my homemade Lemon Concentrate (page 174), but you can also use lemon extract.

Serves 8

For the sponge cake
5 eggs
⅓ cup (70 g) sugar
zest of ½ unwaxed lemon
2 tsp Lemon Concentrate (page 174) or extract
5 tbsp mild olive oil
scant ½ cup (50 g) all-purpose flour

For the cream
Generous 2 cups (500 ml) heavy cream
1 cup (250 ml) plain yogurt
zest of ½ unwaxed lemon
3 tsp Lemon Concentrate or extract
½ cup (60 g) confectioner's sugar, sifted

For the limoncello syrup
2 tsp limoncello
2 tsp water
1 tsp sugar

To decorate
1 lemon, thinly sliced into half moons
fresh mint leaves

Preheat the oven to 350°F (180°C) and lightly grease a 14-inch (36 cm) square baking ban—or you could use a large jelly roll pan or roasting pan. Line with parchment paper.

First make the sponge cake. Separate the eggs into large bowls. Lightly beat the yolks and set aside. Whisk the whites until stiff, then fold in the sugar, lemon zest, and lemon concentrate.

continued on next page...

Gradually fold in the egg yolks, followed by the oil, and then sift in the flour. Pour into the prepared baking pan and bake for 10–12 minutes until golden.

Meanwhile, make the lemon cream. Whip the cream until stiff and combine with the yogurt, lemon zest, and lemon concentrate, then sift in the confectioner's sugar and mix well.

Remove the cake from the oven, turn out onto a wire rack, and allow to cool before carefully removing the parchment paper. Place on a board or work surface lined with a clean sheet of parchment paper and cut into nine 1½-inch (4 cm) strips— keep the strips together for now.

Put the ingredients for the syrup in a small saucepan over medium heat and stir until the sugar dissolves. Remove from the heat and brush the hot liquid all over the cake strips.

Once absorbed, spread some of the cream onto the first strip and carefully roll it up. Place the roll flat in the center of a serving plate. Spread cream on the second strip and roll it around the ready-rolled strip on the plate. Continue doing this until you have used up all the strips so you have one large swirl.

Cover the whole cake with the remaining cream—you could also put some cream in a pastry bag and decorate the cake if you wish. Decorate the top with lemon slices and fresh mint. Chill in the fridge for a couple of hours before serving.

FRAGOLE AL LIMONE E BASILICO
Strawberries with lemon & basil

In Italy, strawberries are often combined with lemon juice. This is a perfect light and healthy dessert in summer when sweet ripe strawberries are in season. You may want to add a little more or less sugar depending on how sweet your fruit is. Serve these with my sorbet (see page 134), semi-freddo (see page 149), ice cream (see page 148), or simply on their own.

Serves 4
14 oz (400 g) strawberries, washed, patted dry, and hulled
2 tablespoons white wine
zest and juice of 1 unwaxed lemon, plus extra zest
    for sprinkling
6 large basil leaves, roughly torn
generous ½ cup (75 g) confectioner's sugar, sifted

In a bowl, combine the strawberries, white wine, lemon zest, and half the basil leaves.

Mix the lemon juice and confectioner's sugar together until the sugar dissolves. Pour over the strawberries, cover, and leave to macerate for about 30 minutes. Serve with the remaining basil leaves and a sprinkling of lemon zest.

CROSTATA AL LIMONE

Lemon tart

I love an Italian crostata like this one with its lattice of pastry strips over the filling. It reminds me of home and childhood when we would often have a slice for *merenda* (afternoon snack). This lemon version is a perfect dessert, on its own or served with mixed berries. Adding zest to the pastry really enhances the lemon flavor.

Serves 8
1 x quantity Lemon Custard (page 188)
egg wash, made with 1 beaten yolk and 1 tbsp milk

For the pastry
2 cups (250 g) all-purpose flour
9 tbsp (125 g) cold butter, cut into small pieces
generous ½ cup (75 g) confectioner's sugar, plus extra to serve
zest of 1 unwaxed lemon
3 egg yolks, lightly beaten

First make the pastry. Sift the flour into a large bowl, add the butter, and use your fingers to rub it into the flour until the mixture resembles breadcrumbs. Sift in the confectioner's sugar and add the lemon zest. Gradually stir in the egg yolks, then mix well with your hands to form a smooth dough. Form into a ball, wrap in plastic, and place in the fridge to rest for at least 30 minutes.

Meanwhile, make the custard. Pour into a bowl, cover, and leave it to cool.

Preheat the oven to 375°F (190°C). Grease and lightly flour an 8½-inch (22 cm) round tart pan.

Unwrap the pastry and transfer to a lightly floured work surface. Roll out to about ¼ inch (5 mm) thick and use to line the prepared tart pan, saving the trimmings. Lightly prick the base with a fork, then pour in the cooled custard.

Gather together then re-roll the pastry trimmings and cut into strips. Arrange over the top to form a lattice pattern. Brush the strips with a little egg wash.

Transfer the tart to the preheated oven, reduce the temperature to 340°F (170°C), and bake for 50 minutes, covering with a loose piece of foil after the first 20 minutes to prevent the custard from browning.

Remove from the oven, leave to cool completely in the pan, dust with confectioner's sugar, and serve.

feuilles de Myrthe
doux

e dite Girosfle Orayuie appel

MOUSSE AL CIOCCOLATO BIANCO E LIMONE CON LAMPONI

White chocolate and lemon mousse with raspberries

This super-easy mousse can be made in no time, requires no cooking, and does not contain eggs. The combination of white chocolate, lemon, and raspberries is perfect and makes a decadent end to a meal, and you could whip this up to serve at parties. It's quite rich, though, so keep the portions small.

Serves 6
½ tablespoon sugar
5½ oz (150 g) raspberries
3½ oz (100 g) white chocolate
1 cup (250 ml) heavy whipping cream
zest of 1 unwaxed lemon and juice of ½

To decorate
raspberries
mint leaves
grated lemon zest

Drizzle the sugar over the raspberries and set aside for about 30 minutes.

Break the chocolate into pieces and place in a heatproof bowl over a pan of barely simmering water. Do not let the water come into contact with the bowl. Leave until the chocolate has melted and then set aside to cool.

Meanwhile, whip the cream until thick. Mash the raspberries with a fork.

Add the lemon zest and juice to the cooled chocolate and fold in the whipped cream until everything is well combined.

Line small glasses with a little of the mashed raspberries followed by a dollop of the creamy mixture. Repeat to make a couple more layers, finishing with the creamy mixture. Decorate each with a whole raspberry, mint leaves, and lemon zest.

Serve immediately or store in the fridge until required.

GELATO AL PARMIGIANO E LIMONE

Parmesan and lemon ice cream

Experimenting with unusual flavors and combining sweet and savory in ice cream is becoming increasingly popular in Italy and Parmesan ice cream can be seen in *gelaterie* (ice cream parlors) up and down the country. Parmesan goes so well with lemon, I thought I would try them together. The combination of slightly salty cheese and tangy lemon is perfect and will surely impress your guests for the perfect dinner party dessert. Simple to make, especially if you have an ice cream machine, but just as easy to make by hand. If you really don't like the idea of adding Parmesan, simply omit it and enjoy a lovely creamy lemon ice cream.

Serves 4–6
3 free-range organic egg yolks
½ cup (100 g) sugar
scant 1 cup (200 ml) heavy cream
scant 1 cup (200 ml) milk, whole or 2%
pared rind of ½ unwaxed lemon
½ cup (60 g) finely grated Parmesan cheese
zest of 2 unwaxed lemons and 4 tbsp juice

Place an empty plastic container or ice cream maker (with a 4-cup/900 ml capacity) in the freezer to chill while you prepare the ice cream.

Beat the egg yolks and sugar together in a bowl until creamy. In a saucepan, combine the cream, milk, and lemon rind and gently bring almost to boiling point. Remove from the heat and beat in the egg mixture. Return to low heat and gently cook, stirring all the time, for 2 minutes. Remove from the heat, discard the lemon rind, and stir in the Parmesan, lemon juice, and lemon zest. Place in an ice cream maker and churn following your machine instructions. Alternatively, make the ice cream by hand as follows:

Take the container out of the freezer, pour in the mixture, and return to the freezer for 30 minutes. After this time, remove the container and beat the mixture well, then return to the freezer and repeat after 30 minutes. Leave in the freezer for 2–3 hours until the ice cream has set, stirring from time to time.

At the end of this time, if the ice cream has set too hard, leave it at room temperature for about 10 minutes to soften before serving.

SEMIFREDDO DI CAFFÈ E LIMONE

Espresso coffee and lemon semifreddo

Semifreddo, which translates as "half cold" is a type of soft ice cream or frozen mousse. Simple to make, without the need to churn, it is a popular dessert in Italy and is often made with mixed berries or nuts. I love the combination of coffee and lemon—I always put a small piece of lemon rind in my espresso—so I decided to make a semifreddo with the same flavors. The slight tang of lemon makes the espresso taste less bitter. It makes the perfect end to a meal. If you love coffee as much as I do, serve this dessert as an affogato—see below.

Serves 6–8
4 tbsp freshly made espresso
zest of 2 unwaxed lemons and 4 tsp lemon juice
scant 1 cup (200 ml) condensed milk
Generous 2 cups (500 ml) heavy whipping cream
lemon rind and coffee beans, to decorate (optional)

First line a 2 lb (900 g) loaf pan with plastic wrap, allowing it to overlap the sides.

Combine the espresso and lemon juice and leave to cool. Then combine with the condensed milk and lemon zest. Whip the cream until stiff. Fold in the coffee mixture until well incorporated. Pour into the prepared pan, cover the surface with the overlapping plastic wrap, and place in the freezer for about 4 hours.

To serve, remove from the freezer, unwrap, and tip out onto a plate. Decorate with lemon rind and coffee beans, if using, and leave at room temperature for about 10 minutes before slicing into portions.

Serve as an affogato by pouring a serving of freshly made sweetened hot espresso over a slab of the semifreddo.

TIRAMISU AL LIMONE

Lemon tiramisu

Here is a lovely refreshing lemon twist to this classic dessert. Savoiardi (sometimes called lady fingers or sponge finger cookies) are dipped in lemon syrup rather than the usual espresso coffee, and lemon zest and a little limoncello flavor the creamy mascarpone. It's a simple dessert, one which can be made in advance and stored in the fridge, and it will surely please everyone. When peeling the lemon, ensure you remove the pith otherwise the syrup could taste bitter.

Serves 4–6
2 eggs, separated
scant ½ cup (80 g) superfine sugar
generous ½ cup (250 g) mascarpone
2 tbsp Limoncello
zest of 1 unwaxed lemon
7 oz (200 g) Savoiardi cookies (lady fingers)

For the lemon syrup
rind and juice of 1 lemon (white pith removed)
scant ½ cup (100 ml) water
¼ cup (50 g) sugar

To make the lemon syrup, place all the ingredients in a small saucepan over medium heat and simmer for 3–4 minutes until the sugar has dissolved and the liquid has reduced slightly. Remove from the heat and leave to cool. Take out the lemon peel, finely chop, and set aside.

Whisk the egg yolks and sugar together until light and creamy. Add the mascarpone and continue to whisk. Stir in the limoncello and lemon zest. In a separate clean bowl, beat the egg whites until stiff, then fold into the creamy mixture and combine well together.

Spread a little of the creamy mascarpone mixture on the base of a serving dish. One by one, quickly dip the cookies into the lemon syrup and put them in the dish to form a layer. Top with more mascarpone, and continue to dip the cookies and build up the layers until the ingredients have all been used, ending with a layer of the mascarpone. Sprinkle the finely chopped lemon rind on top and refrigerate until ready to serve.

DOLCE D'AMALFI
Lemon and almond cake

This cake is the recipe of Salvatore De Riso, a good friend and an excellent pastry chef, from my home village of Minori. He creates the most beautiful cakes using local ingredients, turning them into edible masterpieces. This wonderfully moist and light cake with the delicate taste of lemon and almonds is very simple to make. This cake is usually made in a dome shape, but if you don't have a hemisphere cake pan, a regular 8-inch (20 cm) round one will be fine.

Serves 4–6
Fine semolina, for dusting
9 tbsp (130 g) butter, softened
1⅓ cups (160 g) confectioner's sugar, sifted
zest of 2 unwaxed lemons
2¼ oz (60 g) Candied Lemon Peel (page 158),
   very finely chopped
seeds from ½ vanilla bean
2 large eggs, lightly beaten
1 cup (130 g) all-purpose flour, sifted
1 tsp baking powder, sifted
1 cup (100 g) ground almonds
scant ½ cup (100 ml) milk, at room temperature

To decorate
confectioner's sugar
lemon slices
grated lemon zest

Preheat the oven to 350°F (180°C). Lightly grease an 7-inch (18 cm) hemisphere cake pan (or simply use an 8-inch/20 cm round one) and lightly dust with fine semolina flour.

Cream the butter and confectioner's sugar together until light and fluffy. Add the lemon zest, candied lemon peel, and vanilla seeds. Gradually whisk in the eggs. With a metal spoon, fold in the flour, baking powder, and ground almonds. Gradually add the milk and stir well. Pour the mixture into the prepared pan and bake for 45–50 minutes until risen and golden. Remove from the oven, leave for 5 minutes, then gently turn out onto a plate. When cool, dust with a little confectioner's sugar and decorate with freshly grated lemon zest and a couple of lemon slices.

ZUPPA INGLESE AL CIOCCOLATO E LIMONE

Chocolate and lemon Italian trifle

Zuppa Inglese has nothing to do with soup as its Italian name suggests and I am not sure how it came about, but with custard and sponge fingers, it is very similar to an English trifle. I use the Italian sponge fingers, Savoiardi (lady fingers), in this recipe but you could use leftover pandoro or a plain sponge cake instead.

Serves 6
6 egg yolks
⅔ cup (130 g) sugar
scant ½ cup (50 g) all-purpose flour, sifted
Generous 2 cups (500 ml) hot (not boiling) milk
½ tsp vanilla extract
pared rind of ¼ unwaxed lemon and 4 tsp lemon juice
2 tsp cocoa powder, sifted
7 oz (200 g) Savoiardi biscuits

For the syrup
scant 1 cup (200 ml) water
2 tbsp sugar
3½ tbsp Limoncello (page 166)

To decorate
grated dark chocolate
grated lemon zest

For the syrup, put the water and sugar in a saucepan over medium heat and stir until dissolved. Remove from the heat, pour in the limoncello, and set aside.

In a large saucepan, whisk together the egg yolks and sugar for about 5 minutes until the sugar has dissolved and the mixture is smooth and creamy. Add the flour and continue to whisk until well amalgamated. Whisk in the hot milk, vanilla extract, and lemon rind, then place the pot over low heat, stirring all the time with the whisk or a wooden spoon until it thickens. Remove from the heat and discard the lemon rind. Pour half the custard into a bowl, and stir in the lemon juice. Add sifted cocoa powder to the remaining custard in the pot and mix well until combined.

Dip the cookies into the syrup and use some to line the bottom and sides of a glass serving bowl. Spoon over a layer of the chocolate custard, then lay more soaked cookies on top, then a layer of lemon custard. Repeat the layers, finishing with the lemon custard. Decorate with grated chocolate and lemon zest. Refrigerate until required.

LIMONI CANDITI

Candied lemon peel

When I went to Italy to shoot this book, my friends at Pasticceria Gambardella were making candied lemon and orange peel to sell in their shop. Homemade candied peel is so much tastier (and healthier) than the sugary sticky store-bought variety. The strips of peel can be chopped up and used in cakes or desserts, dipped in chocolate, or eaten as they are for a sweet treat. You can also use oranges and clementines for this recipe. Whatever weight of peel you have, you need equal weights of sugar and water. Don't throw away the rest of the lemon: use the juice for dressings, in cooking, or to make lemon drinks.

Makes 1 x 12 oz (340 g) jar
Peel of 3 lemons—about 4¾ oz (130 g) in weight,
    about ¼ inch (5 mm) thick
⅔ cup (130 g) sugar
generous ½ cup (130 ml) water

Cut the lemon peel into wide strips. Place in a pan and cover with cold water, bring to a boil, and boil rapidly for a couple of minutes. Drain, add fresh water, and repeat this process twice.

After the third time, drain and return to the pan with the sugar and measured water, bring to a boil, and continue boiling until the liquid has evaporated, but be careful not to let it burn.

Remove from the heat, and use a pair of tongs to transfer the peel to a wire rack set over a large dish or tray to catch the excess liquid. Leave to dry out for 2 to 3 days.

Place in an airtight container and use for decoration or flavoring in other desserts. Or dip into melted dark chocolate, allow to dry, and enjoy as a treat.

DRINKS & PRESERVES

GRANITA AL LIMONE DI PAPA' ANTONIO

Lemon granita

Lemon granita is the best thirst-quencher during long hot summer days. This recipe comes from Papa' Antonio, the late father of Sal De Riso, who used to make lemon granita in his tiny cafe in Minori when I was a little boy. I would often watch him zest the lemons and volunteer to help, sinice I knew at the end I would be rewarded with a large glass of ice-cold granita. So simple to prepare, it's worth making a large batch, especially during a heatwave, so you always have something refreshing to enjoy. It's also lovely to add to Valentino's Limoncello Spritz (page 169).

Serves 4–6
zest of 2 unwaxed lemons and
    scant 1 cup (200 ml) lemon juice
1 cup (200 g) sugar
5¼ cups (1.25 liters) very cold water

Strain the lemon juice through a fine sieve into a bowl and add the sugar, stirring until it dissolves. Stir in the cold water and lemon zest. Pour into a container and place in the freezer for 45 minutes. After this time, remove and use a fork to break up the ice crystals. Return to the freezer for 30 minutes and repeat. Do this a couple more times, after which time it should be set, but not hard. Remove and serve in glasses.

If the granita gets too hard, simply leave at room temperature for a few minutes to melt a little and break up the ice crystals with a fork.

LIMONCELLO

This popular after-dinner drink was once only made at home along the Amalfi coast and Sorrento where lemons grow so plentifully. Nowadays, there are many producers who export this liqueur all over the world. I still like to make my own and enjoy the ritual of placing the lemon rinds in a jar with the alcohol. Try to get neutral spirit, which you can buy from specialty stores. As a drink, serve limoncello cold—you can also use it in a variety of desserts.

Makes approx. 5 cups (1.25 liters)
3 unwaxed lemons
generous 2 cups (500 ml) higher-proof grain alcohol (like everclear)
   or 100-proof vodka
generous 3 cups (750 ml) water
2 cups (400 g) sugar

Wash the lemons in cold water, then dry well. Carefully pare off the lemon rind making sure you avoid the white pith. Place the rind in a large jar with airtight lid, pour in the alcohol, and seal well. Place in a cool, dry place for 7 days.

Put the water in a saucepan over the heat and bring to a boil. Add the sugar and stir until it has dissolved. Remove from the heat and allow to cool.

Open the jar and strain the lemon-infused alcohol through a fine sieve, discarding all the peel. Add the alcohol to the sugared water and mix well together. Leave to cool completely, then pour into clean, dry bottles. Seal with lids and store in a cool, dark place for at least 10 days.

LO SPRITZ DI VALENTINO

Valentino's limoncello spritz

This aperitif idea comes from my friend Valentino, who makes his own limoncello from his little factory in Praiano near Positano. Normally this spritz is made simply with one part limoncello and topped up with prosecco, but Valentino also adds one part lemon granita to give it that extra-special refreshing tang. It's an ideal summer aperitif; just make sure you have some lemon granita in the freezer or, if you don't, then simply make it without. And make sure your limoncello and prosecco are well chilled.

Makes 1 champagne flute
1 fl oz (30 ml) limoncello
1 fl oz (30 ml) lemon granita
3½ fl oz (100 ml) prosecco

Pour the limoncello into a champagne flute, or another glass you prefer, add the lemon granita, and top with the prosecco. Serve immediately. *Salute!*

COCKTAIL AL LIMONE
Lemon cocktail

This Campari and lemon cocktail came from the bar at Sal De Riso in Minori. They make lots of different lemon-inspired cocktails, but this is my favorite one. The lemon and sage and Italicus liqueurs can be obtained from good Italian delis or online. Use a cocktail shaker if you have one; if not, just use a cup with a secure lid to do your shaking. If you don't like the idea of raw egg white, then just omit it, but I like the foamy texture it adds to the cocktail.

Makes 2 cocktails
2 fl oz (60 ml) gin
1¾ fl oz (50 ml) lemon & sage liqueur
2 tbsp freshly squeezed lemon juice
½ fl oz (20 ml) Campari
⅓ fl oz (10 ml) Italicus Bergamot liqueur
Ice cubes
1 egg white
2 lemon slices, to garnish

Place all the ingredients except for the egg white and lemon slices into a cocktail shaker and give it a good hard shake for about 30 seconds. Remove the ice cubes, add the egg white, shake again for 30 seconds, and divide between 2 glasses. Garnish with the lemon slices and serve immediately. *Salute!*

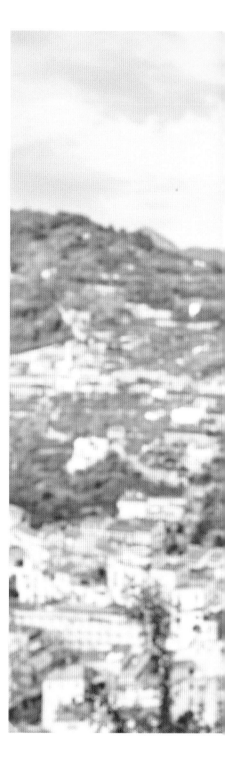

SUCCO DI LIMONE

Lemon concentrate

This healthy homemade lemon syrup is so handy to have for a refreshing drink at any time. You know what's in it, and as it's pure concentrate, you only need a small amount. So when you want a refreshing lemon drink, pour a little into a glass and top up with plain or sparkling water. For anyone with a cold or sore throat, dilute with hot water for a warm soothing drink. You can also make this with oranges, clementines, and even grapefruits.

Makes a generous 2 cups (500 ml)
6 large lemons, squeezed (you need 1½ cups/360 ml juice),
    juice passed through a fine sieve, lemon halves reserved
2¼ cups (440 g) sugar
scant ½ cup (100 ml) water

Put all the ingredients in a saucepan along with 6 lemon halves and bring to a boil. Allow to boil for 10 minutes, stirring from time to time. Remove from the heat, place the lemon halves in a sieve or ricer, and squeeze any juice back into the pan with the rest of the liquid. Then discard the lemon halves. Pour the lemon concentrate into sterilized glass bottle/s, leave to cool, then seal tightly.

Store in the fridge. Once opened it will last for several weeks.

ESPRESSO CON BUCCIA DI LIMONE

Lemon espresso

My day always starts with an espresso to which I like to add a small piece
of lemon rind. It's a habit I picked up from home in Italy; the lemon adds a
refreshing citrus tang to the thick espresso coffee.

Serves 1
Make your espresso in the usual way in your machine. When ready, pour into a cup,
add a small slice of lemon rind, making sure you have no white pith. Stir in sugar to
taste and *buongiorno*!

MARMELLATA DI LIMONI
Lemon jam

Lemon jam is very popular in Italy especially along the Amalfi coast where lemons are plentiful. This really simple recipe, using just two ingredients, will make you want to make your own lemon jam all the time! It's perfect to spread on your morning toast but you could use it to sandwich sponge cakes or flavor desserts. Leaving the lemon slices to soak in water will remove any bitter taste. This keeps well: double or triple the quantities if you wish.

Makes 1 x 12 oz (340 g) jar
1 lb 2 oz (500 g) lemons
1½ cups (300 g) sugar

Sterilize your jar and lid by washing in hot soapy water, rinse then invert onto a baking pan and drying in a preheated oven at 350°F (180°C) for 15 minutes. You can also submerge in vigorously boiling water for 10 minutes. This is not required, but will help the jam keep for longer.

Wash the lemons well under cold running water. Trim both ends of each lemon and thinly slice, removing any seeds. Place the slices in a bowl and cover with plenty of cold water. Cover the bowl and leave for at least 12 hours, changing the water halfway through.

Drain the water, put the lemon slices in a pot, and mix in the sugar. Place over the heat, bring to a boil, and simmer rapidly for 30 minutes. You may want to check it has reached setting point by spooning a little on a cold saucer. If the jam wrinkles when you tilt the saucer, it is ready.

Remove from the heat and use a handheld immersion blender to blend gently so you get a nice combination of smooth jam with bits of peel. Of course, if you prefer it completely smooth, then blend away.

Pour into the sterilized jar, allow to cool completely before covering, and store in the refrigerator. Eat within 3 months.

SAUCES & DRESSINGS

CONDIMENTO ALL'OLIO E LIMONE

Simple salad dressing

A perfect dressing for salads or try it poured over steamed vegetables and fish.

Makes approx. ⅓ cup (90 ml)/Serves 4
4 tbsp extra virgin olive oil
2 tbsp lemon juice
sea salt

Place all the ingredients into a small bowl and whisk for a couple of minutes until creamy. Alternatively put everything in a small bottle or jar, screw on the lid, and give it a good shake before serving.

MAIONESE AL LIMONE

Lemon mayo

I always find delicious, silky homemade mayonnaise much lighter than the store-bought variety. Ensure you buy the best and freshest eggs you can and always use a light olive oil or sunflower oil. As much as I love extra virgin olive oil, it is just too overpowering for a mayonnaise. When you are adding the oil and lemon juice, make sure you add them very gradually: drop by drop is best to ensure you don't split the mayo (you may find you need a little more or less of the quantity of oil specified). For speed, use an electric mixer. Delicious served with simple steamed fish or whatever else you like to serve mayonnaise with. It will keep in the fridge, covered, for about 5 days as long as the eggs you use are fresh and still within their sell-by date.

Serves 2
4 organic free-range egg yolks
pinch of sea salt
6 tbsp light olive or sunflower oil
1½ tbsp lemon juice

Whisk the egg yolks with the salt until well combined. Gradually add the olive oil, drop by drop, while you continue to whisk, until the mixture begins to thicken. At this point, gradually whisk in the lemon juice. Serve immediately or cover and store in the fridge until required.

BESCIAMELLA AL LIMONE

Lemon bechamel sauce

This lemon-infused white sauce combines perfectly with baked pasta dishes that include white fish or veggies such as zucchini, spinach, swiss chard or artichokes. Use this to make Zucchini Lasagne (page 57).

Serves 4
3 tbsp (40 g) butter
⅓ cup (40 g) all-purpose flour
Generous 2 cups (500 ml) milk
zest of 1 unwaxed lemon and juice of ½ lemon
sea salt and freshly ground black pepper
pinch of grated nutmeg

Melt the butter in a saucepan over medium heat, remove from the heat, and whisk in the flour, then gradually add the milk, whisking all the time to avoid lumps. Return to the heat and continue to whisk until the sauce begins to thicken. Remove from the heat, stir in the lemon zest and juice, and season with salt, pepper, and nutmeg. Use immediately or cover and store in the fridge for up to 1 month.

SALSINA ALLA SICILIANA

Sicilian dressing

This Sicilian-inspired dressing can be used warm or cold, poured over steamed fish, on salads, or delicious to dip bread into. If you can find fresh oregano, do use it.

Serves 4
4 tbsp extra virgin olive oil
juice of 1 lemon
½ tsp dried oregano
5 fresh oregano leaves, finely chopped (optional)
½ garlic clove, very finely chopped
pinch of dried red pepper flakes
pinch of sea salt

Combine all the ingredients in a small saucepan over medium heat. Cook, whisking from time to time, for about 5–7 minutes until it begins to thicken slightly.

Remove from the heat and use as desired.

GREMOLADA

This is traditionally the topping for the classic Milanese dish, *ossobuco* (braised veal shanks). But you could also use it to sprinkle on other stews, fish, pasta, or any other savory dishes for a burst of freshness. You could also add a couple of anchovies or, for an extra citrussy taste, some orange zest.

Serves 4
2 garlic cloves, finely chopped
zest of 1 unwaxed lemon
handful of fresh flat-leaf parsley, finely chopped

Combine all the ingredients and use accordingly.

SALSA VERDE AL LIMONE

Lemon salsa verde

Salsa verde is a classic Italian sauce that goes well with meat and fish dishes. I also love it on crostini or simply for dipping in some good bread. It is often made with vinegar, but is equally delicious with lemon juice—and for those who find the taste of vinegar too strong, this is ideal.

Serves 4
1 oz (30 g) crustless stale country bread,
    soaked in a little water
a large handful of flat-leaf parsley
½ garlic clove
1 hard-boiled egg
heaped 1 tbsp salted capers, rinsed
2 anchovy fillets, rinsed if salted
zest and juice of ½ unwaxed lemon
6 tbsp extra virgin olive oil

Use your hands to squeeze out the excess water from the bread, then finely chop. Finely chop the parsley, garlic, egg, capers, anchovies, and the lemon zest. Combine with the lemon juice and olive oil.

Alternatively, if you are in a hurry or prefer a smoother consistency, blend all the ingredients together in a blender or food processor.

SALSA DI BURRO, LIMONE E MENTA

Butter, lemon, and mint sauce

This sauce is ideal for stirring through spaghetti for a quick meal and for more elaborate filled pasta dishes, such as *mezzelune* with lemon and ricotta (see page 52).

Serves 4
7 tbsp (100 g) butter
20 mint leaves
4 tsp lemon juice
scant ½ cup (40 g) grated Parmesan cheese

Put the butter and mint in a frying pan over medium heat and allow the butter to melt. Then add the lemon juice and cook until the butter begins to bubble. Stir in the grated Parmesan. You can now add cooked pasta, loosen with a little of the cooking water, and mix well together. Or use in other recipes.

SALSINA DI ACCIUGHE CAPPERI E LIMONE

Caper, anchovy, and lemon dressing

If you love anchovies, this is the dressing for you! Perfect to pour over steamed white fish or on salads.

Serves 4
4 anchovy fillets
2 tsp capers
5 tbsp extra virgin olive oil
juice of ½ lemon
sea salt and freshly ground black pepper

Very finely chop the anchovies until they resemble a paste. Very finely chop the capers. Set aside.

Whisk the extra virgin olive oil and lemon juice together until it begins to thicken slightly. Stir in the anchovies, capers, and a little salt and pepper to taste—but be careful how much salt you add since the anchovies and capers are quite salty.

Pour into a container and use as required. Before using, give it a quick whisk.

CREMA PASTICCIERA AL LIMONE

Lemon custard

Nothing beats homemade custard once you know how easy it is to make. This delicious lemon custard can be enjoyed as it is, poured over sponge cake, used in trifles, as a sweet tart filling (as in Lemon Tart, page 144) or however else you enjoy custard.

Serves 4–6
6 egg yolks
⅔ cup (130 g) sugar
scant ½ cup (50 g) all-purpose flour
generous 2 cups (500 ml) hot (not boiling) milk
pared rind of ½ unwaxed lemon (without white pith)
2½ tbsp lemon juice

In a saucepan, whisk together the egg yolks and sugar for about 5 minutes until the sugar has dissolved and the mixture is smooth and creamy. Add the flour and continue to whisk until well amalgamated. Whisk in the hot milk and lemon rind, then place the pan over low heat, stirring all the time with the whisk or a wooden spoon, until it thickens. Remove from the heat and stir in the lemon juice.

Serve hot or cold or cover and store in the fridge for up to 3 days. Remember to discard the lemon rind before serving.

INDEX

ACKNOWLEDGMENTS

Liz Przybylski for writing, testing recipes, and organizing me!

Adriana Contaldo for testing recipes and cooking for the shoots.

David Loftus for wonderful photos and lovely days spent in Minori.

Jodene Jordan for beautiful food styling and props.

Penny Forster-Brown for their help at the shoots.

Carmine and Jacopo Porporra for their invaluable help with organizing the shoot in Minori.

Alessandro and Franco Gambardella and their amazing father, Gabriele, who is a master pastry chef and still bakes at his Pasticceria Gambardella in Minori. Also thanks to all his staff at the pastry shop for their help and delicious pastries.

Erminia Carrano for her delicious rabbit dish and to her husband Andrea.

Giuliano and Giuseppe Ruocco for beautiful plates.

Filippo Milo and Fabio for allowing us to shoot at their lovely Orto Paradiso.

Michele Apuzzo the greengrocer and Carlo De Riso of Costagrumi for wonderful lemons.

Giovanni and Antonio Di Bianco and family and all the staff at Giardiniello Restaurant. A special thanks to the chef for creating the beautiful fish dish.

Salvatore de Riso and staff at Sal de Riso for wonderful cakes and cocktails.

Valentino Esposito of Gusto della Costa and his lovely family for their invaluable help and delicious limoncello!

Jamie Oliver for using lemons in his cooking all the time!

Laura Russell, Helen Lewis, Sophie Allen, and Komal Patel at Pavilion.